ATILION

The Hermetic Theurgy to Reveal God Within

New Teurgia: The Path to Christ Consciousness

Contents

About the Author

Since childhood, I have been deeply drawn to the question of what the true nature of the human being is — where the light of consciousness originates, and how we can live in complete harmony with God and the created world. Even as a child, I sensed that behind visible reality there is a deeper, invisible order that permeates and connects everything. This realization was not born from books, but from the longing for inner discovery. A profound spiritual awakening, followed by years of meditation, self-inquiry, and awareness practices, led me to understand that truth is not a theory but a direct experience revealed in the silence of the Soul.

On my journey I experienced the presence of God, saw the light that permeates all forms, and understood the true essence of Jesus' teachings: that the Kingdom of God is within us, not somewhere outside. When the heart is purified, the light begins to shine by itself, and one no longer seeks — one recognizes that they have always been part of the Whole. This experience radically transformed my life, and ever since, I have walked the path of inner silence, contemplative prayer, and mindful presence. Over the years, meditation has ceased to be a practice and has become the natural rhythm of life itself — the Soul's breath within me.

During my studies, I was deeply touched by the Christian mystics — especially Saint Teresa of Ávila, Saint John of the Cross, and Meister Eckhart — as well as by the Hermetic teachings, the Buddhist tradition of mindfulness, and the Taoist philosophy of nature. In these different paths I discovered the same source: the divine consciousness that lives within all beings. I realized that religions and schools may differ outwardly, but in depth they point to the same truth — the realization of love, presence, and inner peace.

For me, the practices of meditation and mindfulness are not merely techniques but new forms of prayer — the wordless prayers of the heart, where we ask for nothing, only *are* in God. Silence is not emptiness but fullness, where thoughts and emotions settle, and in the mirror of the Soul everything becomes clear. Here one understands that prayer does not happen in words, but in presence.

My teachers and masters — among them Yongey Mingyur Rinpoche and Master Richárd Salinger — came from different traditions, yet all pointed to the same realization: the path to the Soul's freedom leads through the understanding of mind and consciousness. Mingyur Rinpoche's teachings helped me recognize the openness and lightness of awareness — the serene wisdom with which we can behold the world without getting lost in it. From him I learned that awareness is not a struggle but a return to our natural state — pure presence. In Richárd Salinger's teachings, recognizing and transforming inner patterns took central place: through understanding unconscious structures and the transformative power of deep meditation, he guided the way back to the integrity of the soul. His practical methods helped me make awareness not an abstract idea but a deep, transforming experience in everyday life.

These masters awakened me to see that the various traditions — whether Christian, Buddhist, Hermetic, or psychological — do not contradict but fulfill one another. Every path leads to the Source, and if we look deeply enough, the heart of Jesus' teaching says the same as the consciousness of Buddha: *Awaken, and know who you truly are.*

The book you now hold in your hands is the fruit of that journey. I did not wish to create a new religion or theoretical system, but to offer a map leading into the heart. The teaching of Jesus and the path of mindfulness are in deep unity — one is the flame of love, the other the light of awareness, and together they illuminate the way. I believe that the practice of awareness, love, and compassion all lead to the living experience of Jesus' heart — the Kingdom of God within. This book is a testimony of that inner path through which the Soul comes to know itself.

Every line I have written was born from personal experience and inner realization. I am not a professional writer; I had never written a book before

— but I felt deeply that I must share what I had received. I wrote this work not as one who *knows*, but as one who *walks the path*: as the light gradually revealed itself, I sought to put into words what I had lived. It surely does not contain the whole of wisdom, but I strove with all my heart to convey the essence — simply, clearly, yet with spirit.

At the end of this book, I have listed suggested readings — works that inspired me most and may help the reader to deepen and grow further. Among hundreds of works I have read on these subjects, these were the most valuable and transformative for me.

This book is for those who feel the call to draw nearer to God, to themselves, and to the Soul; for those who do not seek theory, but Reality — that quiet, radiant Reality that dwells behind every breath.

I wish that this book awakens peace, light, and the joy of presence within you. May it be a companion on your path, a reminder that God is not distant but lives within you — at the stillest point of the heart, where love begins and never ends.

— **Atilion**

Acknowledgments

With a grateful heart, I bow before all who have taught, guided, and inspired me on this path — especially now, as the reader holds these pages in their hands.

Above all, to **Jesus Christ**, who as the living Master within me revealed the way of divine love. Your light is the foundation upon which every realization rests.

Thanks to **God, the Source**, who was present in every step — when I listened to Your call and You spoke to me in silence.

Thanks to the **saints**, all those who, through their faith, love, and courage, showed that darkness cannot overcome light.

I give thanks for the **wisdom of the ancestors**, passed down through generations — the folk tales, the rites, the wisdom that descended into our souls and now returns through this current of remembrance. Gratitude also to the forgotten writers and mystics who dared to give words to divine silence, whether they lived in exile or were silenced — for without you, many true words would have been lost.

I express my heartfelt thanks to the **teachers, masters, guides, and friends** who offered concrete direction when I was lost — those who asked questions, who held up a mirror, who stood beside me amid doubt, fear, and shadow.

I wish to **especially acknowledge Yongey Mingyur Rinpoche**, whose clear-sighted practices and wisdom showed me that the Buddhist path of mindfulness does not contradict Jesus' teachings — it complements them. Through his guidance I came closer to God and to myself, and it became clear how meditation can serve the way of love and devotion.

I also wish to express my gratitude to **Richárd Salinger** — writer, meditation and hypnosis instructor, communication advisor, and mental-health professional — who has woven many teachings into practical methods through his own path. His work, especially his teachings about the mind's patterns and the practices of awareness, resonates deeply with me, helping to understand how the mind functions and how one can step into a higher perspective.

I also wish to express my heartfelt gratitude to my family, who have supported me from the very beginning—guiding me with love and patience, providing all that I needed from childhood to adulthood, and helping me walk this path toward the realization of the Spirit within.

I wish to emphasize that these teachings are not independent from one another but form branches of the same current of light. The Buddhist view does not lessen the authenticity of Jesus' message — it expands understanding: meditation, awareness, and silence are tools through which love and redemption become more tangible in our daily lives.

Just as light does not deny colors, the teaching of Jesus does not deny the true insights of other traditions — all point to the same Source.

I am grateful to **you, dear reader**, for taking this book into your hands — for choosing the journey, the questions, the need for inner vision. I hope what you find within helps you kindle light in yourself, gives you courage for each step, and blesses your life.

Blessings be upon all — upon masters and disciples, old paths and new, light and shadow — for all together write the story of the Soul.

These lines are the breath of gratitude — and the farewell of a living soul that remains forever thankful.

Dedication

I dedicate this book to every seeker — to all who have ever wondered who they truly are.

I dedicate it to those who sometimes feel as though they cannot find their place in this world.

To those who look around and find no answers — neither in the world nor in words.

To those who feel that something essential is missing from their lives, yet cannot quite name what it is.

To those who carry within them a quiet sadness, an inner restlessness, or a deep, wordless longing for something they cannot define.

I dedicate it to those who do not yet understand themselves.

To those who are searching for something, not yet knowing that what they seek is not outside, but within.

To those who sense that beneath the surface of life lies a deeper reality.

And above all, to those who seek God — whether they have walked this path for a long time or are only now beginning it.

To those who wish to draw closer to God, to know His heart — His silent, accepting, and loving presence.

This book is for those who feel that there is *something more*.

For those who know that love is not merely an emotion, but a sacred force that permeates the world.

For those who have begun to sense that God is not a distant, unreachable power, but something that has always been with them — merely veiled by noise, fear, and thought.

This book seeks to help uncover what is already within you: presence. Silence.

Awareness.

And through that awareness — God Himself.

Through these pages, I do not wish to give ready-made answers, but to point in a direction.

A quiet path that does not lead through the noise of the world, but through the stillness of the inner space.

A path that leads to the realization that God is not far away, but very near — so near that He has always dwelt within you.

This path is not easy, but it is profoundly simple.

It demands nothing of you except that you *listen*.

That you *be present*.

That you allow the Reality that has always been there to reveal itself.

This book wishes to be your companion on that journey — to help you awaken to the truth that you are not alone.

That what you seek is not outside, but has always been within you.

That behind sadness there is light.

Behind doubt there is love.

Behind silence there is presence.

And within presence — Christ Himself.

May this book be your companion, your reflection, and your silent witness along the way.

May it help you realize that God does not merely *exist* — He *lives*.

He lives within you.

How to Use This Book

This book is not meant to be rushed through or collected as mere ideas.

It is designed as a lived experience — a gradual unfolding of awareness and inner Presence.

Each chapter reveals a different facet of the same Light.

The reflections offer understanding.

The practices offer transformation.

For the deepest experience, I invite you to move in order — allowing the insights to settle and the meditations to reshape the way you meet each moment. Some practices may call you to pause for a day or a week, as new realizations arise. Honor that.

There is one section in particular you should keep in mind:

Chapter 9 & 10 — Meditative Practices and Daily Meditation Training.

You may choose to continue reading past it when you first arrive there, and return to the practices later.

However, if you wish the realizations in this book to become **more than concepts**, if you wish them to become **living truth** within you, then dedicate **one to two weeks** to each meditation technique presented there.

This is where understanding turns into transformation — where the mind enters silence and the heart opens to what is eternal.

Yet if you feel drawn to continue reading first, follow that inner movement. You can always return to the meditations later — and when you do, return with presence, with openness, and with sincerity.

There is no hurry. This journey meets you exactly where you are. Read with your mind, but listen with your heart. Let the words guide you into Stillness — and let Stillness guide you into God.

Introduction

Dear Reader,

This book does not aim to teach a theory, nor does it merely offer meditation techniques.

It is an invitation — a silent calling, from heart to heart.

If you have ever felt that there is *something more*, something deeper behind life — something unspoken yet strangely familiar — then this book is meant for you.

It does not speak of truths to be found outside yourself, but of what has always lived within you: the eternal, pure awareness.

There is no rush.

There is nothing to prove.

The first pages will not reveal everything.

The answer is not in the opening sentence — but in the silence that lies beneath it.

This path is not difficult — only unfamiliar.

It requires no special ability, only openness.

It does not ask you to become someone else, only to allow yourself to *remember* who you are.

Through the pages of this book, we will step ever more deeply into presence — into that space where thoughts grow still, and something familiar begins to unfold:

the silence that is not empty, but filled with life.

That silence is Christ — the living awareness within us.

Each chapter is not merely something to be read, but a *gate* —

each one an opportunity to pause, to breathe, and to rediscover that the Kingdom of God truly is within you.

So let us begin this journey together.

And let us not hurry to reach the end.

For perhaps the true realization has already been hidden within the very first step.

As you move through these pages, something begins to awaken — not just new knowledge, but the direct experience of peace, clarity, love and divine presence.

Welcome to the path of homecoming.

I

Awakening and the Inner Calling

Dear Reader, dear Seeker,
This book marks the beginning of your journey — the gateway of
inner awakening, where the gentle voice of the Soul first calls to
you. The teachings here are not mere thoughts but living
realizations that can transform your life if read with the heart.
They arise from the wisdom of the ancestors and the Source
within us all —
the indwelling **Christ Consciousness***.*

1

The Beginning of the Inner Path

One moment in my life, I experienced a remarkable, all-encompassing divine radiance. I was neither seeking it nor expecting it — it simply happened. The infinite purity and power of this light awakened such deep reverence and emotion within me that words can barely express it. In that moment, the presence of Love filled everything, and I realized that this Reality had always existed — I was just now able to perceive it.

This experience transformed me. Since then, I have known that all who experience God's light are indeed speaking the truth. Deep within my soul, I understood that when we eventually appear before God, it will not be with our outward selves, but with the awakened presence of our soul.

Since being touched by this light, countless insights and teachings have unfolded within me, gradually transforming my perception entirely. I perceive the world, others, and myself differently. I now share this knowledge and insight — so that those who are ready may recognize the keys to the Kingdom of God, through acceptance, understanding, and realization, and that their hearts may gradually open to the teaching.

For living out the teachings of Jesus Christ is not merely a promise for the future, but is already possible in the present: the divine reality can unfold even now. As we open our hearts to the light, the new Earth is already being born within us.

There comes a sacred moment in every human life when all outer seeking grows weary, and something within calls out: *"Return home."*

This home is not found in the world, but in the innermost sanctuary of the heart — where the soul meets the gaze of God.

For centuries, the Christian mystics have taught that our longing for God is nothing other than God's own attraction toward Himself within us.

It is this inner pull that sets the soul upon its journey — whose first step is the entry into contemplative presence.

This contemplative presence is not a mere technique or lifestyle, but a state of holiness — the silent, wakeful stillness of consciousness,

where everything becomes quiet, yet all phenomena that arise — thoughts, emotions, sensations — are lovingly held,

seen as they appear, abide, and pass away.

And in this stillness of thought, as desires and outer identifications fall away, the Presence of God begins to unfold —

not arriving from elsewhere, but revealing Himself who has always dwelt within.

> **"It is foolish to think that we can enter Heaven without first entering into ourselves."**
> **— Saint Teresa of Ávila**
> The Interior Castle, *Book I*

As Saint Teresa of Ávila said, *"The King dwells within the interior castle."*

Those who enter this castle often at first perceive only a dim light.

The eye of the soul has grown accustomed to the glitter of worldly things, and the inner light — silent, pure, and dazzling in its simplicity — may at first seem strange.

But if attention is steadfast, if the longing is true and burning,

the inner eye of the soul gradually opens.

Here begins awakening — not the acquisition of new knowledge,

but the remembrance of an ancient knowing.

Saint Teresa of Ávila – The Inner Home as a Castle

> **Let nothing disturb you,**
> **Let nothing frighten you;**
> **All things are passing,**
> **God never changes.**
> **Patience obtains all things.**
> **Whoever has God lacks nothing;**
> **God alone suffices.**
> — *Saint Teresa of Ávila*
> (original Latin: "Nada te turbe, nada te espante...") — from The
> Interior Castle

This quotation perfectly expresses that the true home of the soul is not in the changing world, but in the eternal constancy of God.

All worldly things pass away; only God remains — and whoever has Him as their center has nothing to fear, for everything is fulfilled within.

The saints and mystics often spoke of this awakening as an inner transformation.

Saint John of the Cross wrote of *the dark night of the soul*, in which the soul loses everything external it once relied upon, only to discover that which cannot be destroyed.

Suffering, therefore, is not a curse but a mirror — it awakens us to the essential Reality that never fades.

That Reality is God Himself, who is not far away but dwells within us.

In this inner presence, something begins to stir.

We may begin to sense that we are not identical with our thoughts, emotions, or roles.

Something watches, something listens, something simply *is* when all else grows silent.

This awareness is not ours, yet it is our only true Self.

This witnessing consciousness is the gateway to God — indeed, it is the very place where God abides.

As the Apostle Paul says:

> *"Do you not know that you are the temple of God,*
> *and that the Spirit of God dwells in you?"*
> — 1 Corinthians 3:16

This inner experience, in the mystical tradition, is nothing other than **theurgy** — the manifestation of the divine power within our consciousness.

It is not outer ceremonies or rituals that call it forth, but the awake and pure attention of the human being, directed toward God at the deepest point of the soul.

Here, in the silence, the connection is born; here, the Ineffable touches us — the One who does not remain silent.

Theurgy is the living communion between human consciousness and the presence of God.

Here, God does not teach — He *is present.*

He does not give words — He pours forth Being.

He does not reply — He makes us Himself.

This presence does not come from outside, but wells up from within, like a spring that has always been there, only buried.

That spring is none other than the **living presence of Christ within us.**

He is the Word who was with God from the beginning, and who now takes form in our consciousness — if we allow Him.

Thus, contemplative awareness is not only *self-knowledge,* but *God-knowledge.*

True contemplation is always mutual:

God sees the human being, and the human being sees God.

In this gaze, there are no separate selves — only Presence.

This Presence is the Unity itself, where every desire ceases, because all is fulfilled.

On this path we will continue to walk —

step by step awakening the inner witness,

purifying the field of consciousness,

and recognizing the Presence that is already here.
This Presence is our true home —
the inner temple where God dwells *with us* and *within us.*
Here the human soul finds rest, and the heart of the soul whispers:
"Here I am, Lord."

Contemplative Question

"Who is it that arrives home when the seeking falls silent?"

If you say, *"I do,"* then observe — who is this *I* that was once seeking, and
has now arrived?
The body did not move, the world did not change —
and yet, something has returned home.
What is this that is motionless, and yet alive?

**The contemplative questions in this book do not call you to think — they call
you to pause.**

*Do not try to find an answer to them; rather, allow the question to work
within you,*
like a seed germinating in the silence.
Read the question, then close your eyes.
Notice what feeling, thought, or movement arises within you.
Do not judge it — simply be with it.
These questions do not speak to your mind, but to your soul.
And when, at some moment, there is only silence,
you will know that the answer is already there —
not in words, but within you.
Do not analyze — listen.

2

Awakening into Presence

There are moments in life when everything falls silent.
When, for an instant, the noises of the outer world fade away,
and we sense that something is *watching within us.*
It is not the familiar thinking self,
not the roles we carry —
this watcher is deeper.
Vaster.
Timeless.
It does not seek reasons,
it desires nothing —
it simply *is present.*

This presence is not something we must attain —
it is something we return to.
For life does not wish to teach us from the outside,
but to remind us from within who we truly are.

Most people spend their whole lives upon the stage of thought —
actors in their own story,
lost in memories of the past and worries of the future,
in the whirl of judgment and desire.

And in the midst of it all — unnoticed —
we drift away from the sacredness of the present moment.

Yet the *Present* is the only place where God is available.
    Not in the past — for it is gone.
    Not in the future — for it has not yet come.
    Only *now*.
    Here.
    In this very moment —
    where the breath happens,
    where the heart beats,
    where silence speaks.

This Presence — this conscious, open awareness —
    is none other than the **Christ living within you.**
    Not metaphorically, not as a theological concept —
    but as reality itself.
    The awareness that does not judge.
    The attention that excludes nothing.
    The Presence that embraces everything.
    This is the Divine Consciousness that Jesus realized within Himself —
    and that you, too, can rediscover within yourself.

Jesus did not only teach that God loves —
    He taught that *God is within you.*
    "The Kingdom of God is within you."
    This is not abstract philosophy —
    it is direct experience.
    An experience that unfolds
    when we cease to follow our thoughts
    and simply *are present.*

But how can we return to this Presence?

First, we notice that we are *not* present —
that we have become lost in the past or the future,
that our body is here, yet our attention scattered.
This is the first step — not blame, but awakening.
And when we notice this, we can return —
to the breath,
to the sensations of the body,
to the sounds,
to reality itself.

And in that return, something opens: *silence.*
Not an empty silence —
but a living, alert, divine stillness.
This is the silence where Jesus dwells —
not in a loud external temple,
but in the inner sanctuary of the soul.
There, where there are no thoughts — only awareness.
Where there is no judgment — only acceptance.

This Presence is not a goal to reach —
it is the starting point.
Every practice, every meditation, every prayer leads back here.
For we do not pray to come closer to God,
but to realize that He is already here —
behind every thought,
beneath every feeling,
before every movement.
He is the Presence through which all things exist.

Thus, the practice of presence is not a technique —
it is *homecoming.*
Attention is not a tool —
it is a gift.

When you are attentive,
the Divine Consciousness is attending to Itself.
And that moment — no matter how ordinary —
becomes sacred.

The Christian mystics — Teresa of Ávila, Meister Eckhart,
and John the Evangelist — knew this.
They did not merely believe in Jesus —
they recognized Him *within themselves:*
the living Christ within,
not as a separate being,
but as their true divine nature.
This realization is not arrogance — it is humility.
For it does not say, "I am God,"
but "Christ lives in me."
And this makes every human being equal before God.

Thus begins awakening —
not through miracles or visions,
but through simple awareness.
You grow still.
You seek nothing —
and yet, you find everything.

This book does not call you to believe what it says —
but to *remember* what you already know.
Not to learn new words,
but to feel the ancient truths
that have always lived within you.

In Presence, the path opens.
And this path leads nowhere else but *here* —
into the moment where God is already present.

Where Christ does not approach from without,
but calls to you from within.
And where there are no more questions —
only gratitude.
For you have arrived home —
to yourself,
and in Him.

Contemplative Question

"When everything falls silent within you — who is it that still hears the silence?"

3

The Language of the Soul: Contemplative Awareness

Attention is not merely a mental function — attention is the **language of the Soul.**

Where there is attention, there is presence.

Where there is presence, there is love.

And where there is love, there God Himself is present.

It is no coincidence, then, that contemplative awareness is the foundation of every genuine inner path.

Modern human attention is scattered in a thousand directions.

We have grown used to attaching ourselves constantly to outer stimuli — to screens, thoughts, emotions, plans.

Our attention is often not our own; it is seduced by advertising, fears, and desires.

But the Soul does not speak where there is noise.

The Soul whispers — and can only be heard when we quiet the heart.

Contemplative attention is not effort. It is not concentration.

It is more like allowing and accepting —

like listening to someone you love deeply: you do not wish to add anything, only to receive.

This is how we are invited to look upon the world and upon ourselves.

Not to "understand" or "change" everything —
but to allow it to *be*, so that it may reveal itself as it is.
This kind of attention is gentle and open.
It does not evaluate or categorize.
It does not call anything "good" or "bad."
It simply *sees.*
And just as Jesus looked upon others — something begins to look through you as well.
Not from the outside, but from within:
the pure awareness — **the gaze of Christ within you.**

Attention as Prayer

Contemplative attention is not only a practical tool — it is **prayer.**

A wordless form of communion, in which we do not speak *to* God, but *are with* God.

Like sitting beside someone you love — there is nothing to say, for presence itself speaks.

When this attention is pure, it is directed toward God even when observing the breath or a simple sound.

For everything that you contemplate with full openness reveals the features of God.

You need not focus only on "holy" things for your attention to become sacred.

Washing dishes, walking, hearing a bird's song, feeling your body move — all can become icons when you are present.

Everything can become prayer when your focus rests not on a goal, but on reality itself.

The Christian contemplatives have always known this.

Mother Teresa once said:

"God does not ask us to be successful, but to be faithful."
Attention is this inner faithfulness — the choice not to abandon the moment, no matter what happens.

The Movement of the Soul

As you continue to practice present, aware attention, you will begin to notice something profound:

it is not *you* who pays attention — something deeper is aware *through you*.

A quiet intelligence.

A gentle, wise consciousness.

And this is none other than **the living Christ within.**

Not the learned image of faith, not a religious icon,

but the living awareness that simply *is*, beholding all things with love.

This attention does not strain, does not tire, and cannot be broken —

for it is not human.

It is the movement of the Spirit within you —

the Consciousness that transcends all things and yet permeates everything.

And if this is so, then in every moment of true attention

you are participating in divine life itself.

You are not merely an observer —

you are a participant in the radiance of God.

This is what the heart already knows,

and what the mind gradually learns to follow through practice.

(This is for Advanced Meditators)

Practice – Contemplative Attention

Sit down in a quiet place.

Find a posture that is comfortable, yet alert.

Bring your attention to the present moment — to sounds, bodily sensations, the rhythm of your breath.

Seek nothing. Simply *observe*.

If a thought arises, recognize it: *"This is a thought."*

Then gently return to direct experience.

Remain in this open awareness for 5–10 minutes.

Finally, say quietly within yourself:

"I am here. You are here too."

As attention becomes purified, our vision also clears —

and we slowly realize that the world does not separate us from God,
but leads us back to Him.
In every moment of true awareness, we arrive —
not only into the present, but into the **Presence of God.**

Contemplative Question

"When you are attentive — who is it that is aware?"

4

Awareness as the Gateway

The Observing Self: The First Light of Sacred Presence

E very true transformation begins with a single moment — the moment when one no longer observes *things*, but the one who observes.

The watcher of attention, the radiant light of consciousness, is not a created thing — it is **Presence** itself.

For centuries, many have sought God in words, rituals, and thoughts.

But God does not dwell in what can be conceived.

God is the Pure Reality that exists before every thought and beyond every form.

The Silence Behind Thoughts

Consciousness is not a product of the mind.

It is not a refined form of thinking, but the very *light* in which thoughts appear.

This light is not of worldly origin; it is the radiance of the **Word before creation**,

the unveiled face of Christ.

For when consciousness perceives purely, God gazes through it.

This awareness is not something we possess —
it is what we *are*, before we think anything about ourselves.

The Light of the Word: Christ's Presence in Consciousness
Mystics have often spoken of this inner seeing.
It does not see with bodily eyes, but through the light of God.
As Meister Eckhart said:

> *"The eye with which I see God is the same eye with which God sees me."*
> *This is not poetry, but realization —*
> *for when one awakens to awareness, one recognizes that the seer is not the "me,"*
> *but the **I Am**.*

The gate of consciousness does not open with trumpets,
but with intentional attention — receptive and yielding.
It is opened not by mapping the way, but by surrender.
We let go of control, of the need to know, of the desire to be worthy,
and simply remain present — accepting the moment as it is,
without identifying with what arises,
knowing that our true being — the pure, seeing awareness —
is God's outpouring into the world,
where Jesus and the true Self become one.

1. Jesus: "I Am in Them"

> *"I in them, and You in Me, that they may be made perfect in one;*
> *and that the world may know that You have sent Me,*
> *and have loved them, as You have loved Me."*
> — John 17:23

Here, in His High Priestly Prayer, Jesus clearly declares that He Himself is within people, and the Father is within Him — revealing that divine unity may be realized in every human being.

This presence is not idle emptiness but **fertile awareness** —
like the heart of the Virgin Mary, who sought not to possess, but to receive.
In this receptivity, the gate opens:
something begins to shine in consciousness —
not of this world, yet deeply real.
A divine gentleness permeates everything,
wishing to be nothing other than what it already is.
This is the **Presence of Christ within us** —
not a form, not a concept,
but the living Word who has always been here.

The Return: Consciousness as Homecoming

This realization is **theurgy itself.**
In awareness, we do not merely become observers — we become temples.
The light we behold awakens to life within us.
God does not look upon us from afar;
He recognizes His own light through our contemplative awareness.
This mystery is not a promise of the future,
but the reality of the present moment.
Thus, consciousness as the gate is not a doorway *to somewhere*,
but a return to where we have always been — **the heart of God.**
Every act of contemplation, every moment of inner attention, leads to this
recognition:
that what we sought has always been within us —
and that the one who was seeking was God Himself within.
For the true seeker is not the small self,
but the **I Am**, eternally returning to Itself.
In the next chapter, we will explore the deeper nature of this awareness —
how it functions, how it becomes veiled,
and how it can be purified again
so that we may become living temples of the divine.
When consciousness recognizes itself,

the divine light is reborn in the human being.

This is what the ancient Hermetic sages called **"the Return of the Light"**
—

the moment when the Formless shines through form,

and the divine awareness awakens within humanity once more.

For the light has never vanished —

we have only forgotten that it flows from within us.

5

Christ Within: The Incarnation of the Word in Consciousness

The Inner Word: Presence Without Beginning

"In the beginning was the Word," says the Gospel of John.
This *beginning* is not a moment in time, but an eternal reality:
at the heart of Being shines the Divine Word — the *Logos* — through whom all things came to be.

This Word is not only the speech that created the world;
it is also the echo resounding in the depths of every soul, whispering in each moment:

"Be who you are."

Christ, the Word, did not appear only in a single historical person,
but dwells as an eternal Presence in the depths of every human being.
When the mind grows silent and the heart begins to listen,
this inner Word speaks again — not in language, but in *being*;
not through teaching, but through *existence*.
Whoever listens in silence hears it;
whoever gazes with humility perceives it.

Christ Taking Form in Consciousness
Many believe that Christ "comes" from without —
but the mystic knows that the true coming of Christ happens *within.*
As the Apostle Paul wrote:

"It is no longer I who live, but Christ who lives in me."

This is not metaphor but literal divine reality.
The Word becomes flesh *in consciousness* when consciousness releases itself
and opens to the Being of God.
In this inner incarnation, it is not that Christ somehow *enters* the human being —
rather, the human fades away, and only Christ remains.
Thoughts cease, will falls silent, desires dissolve,
and what remains is the pure **I Am** —
that which has always been in God from the beginning.

Consciousness: The Dwelling of the Holy Spirit
The Holy Spirit is not merely a "person of the Trinity,"
but the living divine Breath — pervading space, time, and consciousness.
When a person enters the contemplative silence, they are not alone there.
It is the Spirit who prays within them,
the Spirit who recognizes Christ,
and the Spirit who utters the unutterable.
Thus we may say that **consciousness is the holy place**
where the Son is incarnated and the Spirit is present.
Consciousness is not neutral space — it is *sanctuary:*
the temple in which the glory of God dwells.
And whoever enters it — with the nakedness of pure attention —
becomes themselves a Word:
God's spoken life made visible in the world.

The Mystery of Transformation

Christ within us does not remain a passive light.
Whoever receives Him is transformed.
Not into a *better* human being, but into a *new* one.
Not more moral, but more divine.
The true Christian path is not a change of behavior,
but a **change of being** —
the awakening of the divine *I Am* within human consciousness.
This transformation does not occur by our own power.
There is no technique that can produce it.
There is only one way: **surrender.**
When one relinquishes everything — even the desire to attain anything —
then the gate opens, and the Word becomes flesh within.
This is the deepest level of theurgy:
God becomes His own Presence within us,
and we become His consciousness in the world.

Living in Christ: The New Order of Inner Life

One who recognizes Christ within no longer lives as before.
They do not walk by the laws of the world,
but by the inner light.
This inner life is quiet, humble, and yet immense.
It does not strive, it *radiates.*
It does not seek to prove, it *reflects.*
It does not boast, for it knows:

"What I see is not myself — but Him who lives in me."

The order of the inner life is not hierarchy, but *flow;*
not domination, but *receptivity.*
It is Christ's Presence that renews all things.
And whoever lives in this Presence
becomes the light of the world —
without ever trying to be so.

6

Inner Guidance: Hearing the Voice of the Spirit

The Spirit Does Not Speak from Outside

Those who listen in silence long enough eventually recognize this: the guidance they have been seeking does not come from without. The Spirit is not loud, commanding, or argumentative.

He is gentle — like a breath.

Like the wind of which Jesus spoke:

> *"You do not know where it comes from or where it goes, but you hear its sound."*
>
> *This sound is not heard with the ear, but felt as a trembling in the depths of the heart.*

Inner guidance does not unfold on the level of thoughts.

It moves not *between* words, but *beneath* them.

The Spirit does not explain — He shows.

Sometimes in a gesture, a feeling, or an unexpected peace.

At other times, He is simply present in silence, doing nothing, yet being all.

Thus, hearing is not strained attention but surrendered presence —

like a lake whose ripples have stilled, allowing the depths to reflect the sky.

Whoever *tries* to hear, will not.

But whoever allows hearing to happen — will hear.

The voice of the Spirit cannot be produced,

but one can open to it.

Just as we cannot command the wind to move,

but we can open the window to let it pass through the room.

So it is with the Spirit: He cannot be controlled,

but He can be invited — through attention and humility.

Hearing, then, is not an action, but *receptivity*.

Recognizing Inner Answers

Many ask: *How do I know that what I feel is truly the voice of the Spirit, and not my mind?*

The answer is not intellectual.

The presence of the Spirit brings peace — not always comfort, but peace.

A decision, a direction, or an insight is authentic when, deep within, something *rests* in it.

This peace is not the peace of fulfilled desires,

but the stillness of God's presence.

It may not come with emotion or euphoria,

but as a quiet "yes" — an inner confirmation that does not shout, but abides.

When the Spirit reveals something, it is never forceful.

It does not pressure or persuade.

It is like a door that opens suddenly where once there was a wall.

The Spirit does not argue — He simply shows.

We are rarely given the whole picture, only the *next step.*

But that step is clear, gentle, and without coercion.

Inner guidance often does not *speak* — it *unfolds:*

as the path appears under our feet

just when we thought there was no way forward.
And as we step, the next step reveals itself.
The Spirit's answers do not arise from logic
but from the depth where God dwells within us.
Therefore, we are not meant to *seek* answers, but to *notice* them.
Sometimes the answer comes immediately after the question,
other times days later, in an unexpected moment.
What matters is not to "hear correctly,"
but to remain *openly present.*

The Practice of Trust

Following inner guidance is rarely accompanied by certainty —
but always by **trust.**
We often do not know where the path leads;
we only sense that we are called to take this next step now.
Thus, the contemplative life is not control but surrender.
When the Spirit leads, things often do not go as planned —
but exactly as needed for the ripening of the soul.
This path is like walking in fog:
we cannot see the destination, only the next step.
Such trust is not blind faith; it is born of experience.
Those who follow the inner voice of stillness again and again
discover that it always leads them where God awaits.
Not always to the easiest road —
but always to the deepest one.
Trust also means allowing ourselves to err.
Sometimes in listening to the Spirit, we set out upon a way
that later proves not to have been the best direction.
But even from this, God brings forth life.
Trust means not fearing mistakes —
knowing that the Spirit does not seek perfection,
but openness and willingness.
Guidance, therefore, is not a sequence of flawless choices,

but a living relationship in which God walks with us.

Practical Exercise – Listening to the Spirit

Find a quiet place where you can sit undisturbed for a few minutes.

Sit upright yet relaxed, and close your eyes.

Bring your attention to your breathing —

do not alter it, simply follow it as it enters and leaves.

Allow your mind to rest in this rhythm for 3–5 minutes.

Then, when you feel settled, gently ask within:

"What is the Spirit inviting me to now?"

Do not think about it or answer immediately — just listen.

A word, an image, a memory, a bodily sensation,

or a gentle sense of presence may arise.

Remain open.

If nothing comes, do not force it.

The Spirit often responds with silence.

This practice is not about manufacturing answers,

but about learning to listen.

Repeat it regularly, and guidance will become more natural.

You may wish to write down what you experience —

but always add the words:

"Thy will be done."

For the deepest guidance is always that

which leads us back into the **Presence of God.**

7

The Hermetic Voice: The Primordial Source of Theurgy

"He who knows himself knows the All."
— Corpus Hermeticum, X

T he word *Theurgy* comes from the ancient Greek θεουργία, meaning
"the work of God" or *"divine action."*
Those who first used this word were not referring to rituals,
but to an inner, sacred process — the moment when a person no longer
acts by their own will,
but when **God acts through them.**
This realization was one of the deepest teachings of the ancient Hermetic
writings — the *Hermetica*.
The Hermetica was not a religion, but an *inner path* to divine knowing.
According to **Hermes Trismegistus — the "Thrice-Great" —**
the human being is a divine being who has forgotten their own light
and now journeys home to the Source.
This return does not occur through outward travel,
but through the transformation of consciousness:

"Light is the Mind of God, and whoever knows the Light knows God."
— Corpus Hermeticum, *XI*

In this ancient wisdom, *Theurgy* names the state in which the soul of man
and the Spirit of God become one in silence —
when action no longer arises from the individual, but from the Whole.
This is not mere philosophy, but mystical experience —
the same truth Jesus expressed when He said:

"I am in the Father, and the Father is in Me."

The New Theurgy – The Path of the Christ Within

The *New Teurgia* — whose teachings are contained in this book — is not a
new religion,
but the rebirth of the divine-human unity in **conscious presence.**
This path does not seek God from without,
but reveals Him from within — through silence, attention, love, and
surrender.
The *New Teurgia* is new not because of doctrine,
but because the focus has shifted from *human effort* to **divine self-
revelation.**
It is not magical theurgy, but **graceful theurgy** —
where the human being does not invoke God,
but recognizes Him within and allows God to act through them.

"Theurgy unites the divine and the human so that the soul becomes
a co-worker of God."
— Iamblichus, De Mysteriis

Thus, the *New Teurgia* is not humanity's path to God,
but **God's path within humanity.**
It finds its fulfillment in **Christ Consciousness** —

when one realizes they are not a separate being,
but an expression of God's own consciousness within creation.
This book speaks of that path —
of the recognition of the inner Light,
of the transfiguration of consciousness,
and of the grace in which God finally recognizes Himself *within you.*

  "Man is God's Word in the world.
    When silence speaks within him,
    God hears Himself."
    — Atilion, New Teurgia

The Ancient Theurgy – The Practice of Divine Union

In the early Hermetic and Christian communities, *theurgy* was not the performance of outer rituals or invocations.

It was the sacred art of inner transformation — the awakening of the divine presence within the soul.

The ancient sages of Alexandria and the early Christian mystics understood that the true temple of God is not made by human hands,

but is the living heart purified by love and silence.

The Hermetic masters taught that the purpose of life is to remember our divine origin and to allow the *Nous*, the Divine Mind, to shine through us.

Their contemplative practices were acts of inward ascent — prayers without words, meditations upon the Light — through which the soul aligned itself with the Divine.

When the human will became still and transparent, the divine action (*theourgia*) could move through it.

This was not self-glorification, but self-emptying — the same mystery Christ revealed in His own life and prayer:

"Not my will, but Thine be done."

Many of the first Christian contemplatives — in Egypt, Syria, and Cappadocia — practiced a living form of theurgy.

They entered silence, surrendered the personal will, and let the Spirit pray within them.

What they called *hesychia* — the stillness of the heart — was in truth the same divine operation known to the Hermetic masters.

Through this inner stillness, God's light was not worshipped as distant, but realized as immanent:

the divine Word (*Logos*) speaking from within the soul.

Thus, the ancient theurgy was the sacred cooperation between God and man,

where prayer became union, and action became the movement of the Divine through creation.

The New Teurgia - The Rebirth of Christ Within

The New Teurgia is not a return to ancient rites,

but the renewal of their inner essence in the light of Christ-consciousness.

It restores the forgotten experience that divinity is not to be sought beyond the world,

but discovered within the depth of one's own being.

In this path, the soul no longer strives to reach God through effort,

but allows God to reveal Himself through presence.

The divine action is no longer something we perform — it is what happens when we cease to interfere.

When the mind becomes silent, the heart open, and attention steady,

the Logos — the living Word — begins to act through us once again.

This is the same realization the early followers of Jesus experienced in their hearts:

that *Christ in you is the hope of glory* — the inner anointing through which divine and human become one.

The New Teurgia is therefore not a new belief, but a remembrance of the original Christian revelation:

that every human being is a vessel of divine light.

When this awareness awakens, love becomes unconditional,

forgiveness becomes spontaneous,

and every act becomes an expression of divine harmony.

The soul no longer seeks miracles — it becomes the miracle itself.

The Hermetic writings foresaw this time,

when humanity would rediscover the divine presence not through religion,

but through direct experience.

In the silence of the heart, the Word once again becomes flesh.

This is the New Teurgia —

the living realization that God acts, speaks, and loves within you.

8

The Way to Silence

The world is noisy — not only outwardly, but within. The stream of thoughts, the flow of emotions, the restless inner commentator — together they form the mental stage upon which we have played for so long.

Most people never notice that all this is merely background noise — and behind it lies something far deeper: **silence.**

But not just any silence.

Not the absence of sound, but the **pure presence of consciousness** — untouched by anything.

This silence is not empty; it is *awake.*

And this silence — in Jesus' words — is the *"secret place"* where the Father *"sees in secret."*

It is not to be found outside. It is within you.

When we first begin to observe our inner world, we often feel disappointed: we do not find silence, but more noise.

This is natural.

When the surface stills, the sediment rises.

But if we persist, something begins to settle — like muddy water clearing as the sand sinks to the bottom.

Then, slowly, the inner space becomes visible.

This space is not part of our personality.

It is not the mind, nor the emotions, nor the body —
but *that which observes them all.*
This witnessing presence does nothing, yet simply *is.*
And in this "just being," something becomes sanctified — not because it is special, but because it is **real.**

Silence Is Not Attained — It Is Recognized

Many seek silence as if it were something to achieve.
But silence is not a goal.
Silence is not something we *reach* — it is something we *discover.*
It has always been there; we simply did not notice.
Silence is not new — noise was temporary.
Thus, we do not come to silence by suppressing noise,
but by observing.
The moment you observe — not with effort, but with openness and acceptance — silence reveals itself.
Silence is not the object of attention — **attention itself is silence.**
The deepest silence is not the absence of sound, but the *space in which everything appears.*
And that space is the **Christ Consciousness** living within you.

Silence: The Temple of the Spirit

Christian mysticism has always known this inner silence —
not as muteness, but as a loving, alert presence beyond words and forms.
This silence is not impersonal — it is the **realm of the Holy Spirit.**
It is here, in this silence, that the encounter happens —
not in imagination or thought, but in *Presence.*
In *The Interior Castle*, St. Teresa of Ávila called this the innermost chamber
—

the room of total silence, where the soul unites with God.
And this is not an abstraction; it happens whenever we simply rest in God's Presence, desiring nothing else.
Jesus Himself often withdrew to be *"alone with the Father."*

Why?

Not to gain something — but to return into that living relationship where separation ceases.

This silence is not inactivity — it is *being in love.*

Silence Holds Us

As we continue to practice presence, we discover that silence does not depend on us.

Silence is not there *because* we meditate well —

it is there because **God has always been present.**

Noise merely obscures it.

Attention does not create silence — it allows us to perceive it.

And once we perceive it, something changes.

Thoughts no longer dominate; emotions no longer rule.

A deeper foundation emerges — the silence born of Spirit.

This silence sustains us, like an inner rock unmoved by outer storms.

It is refuge — the tangible yet unspeakable space of divine Presence.

Practice – Discovering Silence

Sit quietly, comfortably, yet alert.

Close your eyes and simply *observe.*

Do not seek silence — just notice what is.

If there is noise, listen to it.

If there is thought, allow it.

Do not react. Just remain.

Notice the space in which all noise appears.

That space *is* silence.

Rest in it for a few minutes.

When you rise, say quietly within:

"The silence has not vanished — I have returned to it."

This silence is not bound to special moments.

It does not require a monastery, nor perfect calm.

It is always here — waiting for us to pause and observe.

For silence is nothing less than **the Presence of God within.**

And in that Presence, every question fades —

not because it is answered, but because it is no longer needed.

In silence, all can be found — not as information, but as **peace, love, and being.**

Whoever rests in this silence no longer searches,

for they have realized: **God does not come — God is already here.**

Do not cling to this silence; rather, recognize it **between two thoughts.**

Then, allow whatever arises to arise.

Practice divine acceptance.

And when it passes, recognize again the silence —

and *that which recognizes the silence:*

the **Pure Awareness, your true Self, the outpouring of God.**

See this Presence in all things —

for everything appears *in it* because you are *Presence itself.*

II

Purification and Transformation

9

Meditative Practices

Entering the Practice – Where Transformation Begins

Y ou have now arrived at the heart of this journey.
Everything you have read so far has prepared the mind —
but here, the mind must become silent and allow Presence to reveal itself.

The meditations in this chapter are not optional decorations.

They are the gates through which the teachings become **your living experience**.

To step through each gate, patience and rhythm are essential.

Dedicate one to two weeks to each technique before moving to the next.

I will also provide a suggested timeline to guide you along this path.

Practice **every day**, at a **specific time** you choose in advance.

The time matters — it anchors your intention in the structure of your life and signals to the mind: *this moment is set apart for transformation.*

As you explore each practice, let it shape the way you see, feel, and respond.

Stay with it long enough for it to touch your daily life,

for that is when the real shift occurs.

Once you are familiar with all techniques,

you may begin to **interweave them**:

- One day this practice, another day that
- Or two shorter meditations back-to-back
- *(for example: 15 minutes + 15 minutes)*
- Follow what brings you closer to Presence

This chapter is not merely the middle of the book.

It is the **threshold** — where knowledge dissolves into Presence,
and Presence reveals what has always been true.
Let every breath here be a step through that threshold.
Your only task: **show up** — fully and sincerely.

The Art of Meditation – From the Recognition of Consciousness to Deep Awareness

The true essence of meditation is not technique, but **recognition** — *being aware that you are aware.*

This is the beginning of awakening, the moment when consciousness recognizes itself.

From here every path unfolds — whether it is observing bodily sensations, listening to sounds, noticing thoughts, or resting in open awareness.

The aim is simply to return to what has always been here: the state of **pure presence.**

The Principles of Meditation - Mindful Presence and Acceptance

True meditation is not an escape from thoughts or emotions,

but **alert presence within them.**

Its foundation is mindful awareness — recognizing what is happening here and now

without trying to change or reject it.

This attitude heals both mind and body,

for the struggle with "what is" comes to rest.

Consciousness does not try to control experience;

it opens to it with curiosity and gentleness.

Meditation is presence, acceptance, curiosity, and kindness.

Presence means that attention rests in the now — not in the past, not in the future.

Acceptance means that whatever arises — a thought, a feeling, a sensation — is allowed to be.

Kindness means treating yourself and others with compassion throughout the process.

Together, these create the inner space where healing and awakening can unfold.

Practice

Sit comfortably and bring your attention to the breath.

Do not try to control it — simply notice it.

When the mind wanders, recognize it and return to the breath —
not with judgment, but with kindness.

if you cant be kind that is okay too just see the judgment appears.

you can say to your self "i see judgment appeared".

When pain, tension, or a difficult emotion arises, do not resist it.

Say quietly within: *"It's okay that this is here."*

This is the moment of befriending yourself.

Through the practice of mindful attention,

you begin to see that thoughts, feelings, and bodily sensations
are like waves on the ocean of consciousness.

They come and go naturally — there is no need to fight them.

Right meditation is not about achieving a goal,

but about learning to rest in aware, kind presence —
the beginning of true freedom.

Everyday Practice

Choose a few simple moments during the day — eating, walking, showering
—

and be fully attentive to what you are doing.

Feel the taste, the movement, the touch of water.
When attention drifts, simply return.
This ordinary mindfulness cultivates the same awareness
as seated meditation.

Meditation thus becomes a path of **self-acceptance and pure presence.**
There is nothing to achieve — only to arrive in what is already here.
Beyond the silence of attention lies freedom, kindness, and deep peace —
qualities that have always belonged to the very nature of consciousness.

Curiosity as the Heart of Meditation

Curiosity is one of the deepest keys to awakening.
In childhood it was naturally alive within us —
every sound, color, scent, and movement was new.
In meditation, we return to this pure, open attention.
We do not sit to "do it right,"
but to **discover what is truly happening right now.**
When we turn toward experience with curiosity,
the judgment of good or bad dissolves.
Pleasant sensations cease to be goals,
and unpleasant ones are no longer enemies.
We simply observe:
"What is this feeling? Where does it appear? How does it change?"
Curiosity becomes transformation:
resistance turns into interest,
fear into exploration,
habit into living presence.
This attitude opens consciousness to grace —
for one who is truly curious no longer seeks to possess,
but only to see truth as it is.

As **Jesus** said:

"Seek, and you shall find."
The spirit of seeking does not arise from lack,
*but from the **eternal curiosity of the Spirit***
that longs to recognize itself in all things.

The Principles of Posture – The Foundation of Mindful Presence

In meditation, posture is not merely an external form —
it is the physical foundation of mindful presence.
The body supports the mind in remaining both alert and at ease.

1. The Way of Sitting
Sit in a stable yet comfortable position.
You may sit cross-legged on a cushion or on a chair if that is easier.
The key is that the body supports itself without constant adjustment —
so that attention can remain free.

2. Legs
If sitting on the floor, cross the legs so that both knees are close to the
ground.
This creates a stable three-point foundation — the sitting bones and the
knees.
If sitting on a chair, place both feet flat on the floor,
knees roughly at right angles, feet parallel.
This grounded base gives rise to the natural upward lift of the spine.

3. Spine
Keep the back straight but not rigid.
Imagine a thread gently drawing the crown of your head upward —
this creates a natural vertical alignment that awakens alertness.
Too relaxed, and the body tends to drift into drowsiness;

too tense, and it breeds strain.
Find the balance between alertness and ease.

4. Shoulders and Arms

Let the shoulders release naturally downward.
Rest the hands on your thighs or in your lap,
palms facing down or up — whichever feels comfortable.

5. Head and Face

Let the head tilt slightly forward, the chin gently lowered.
The eyes may be closed or softly open,
the gaze resting lightly without focus.
Relax the muscles of the face — especially the forehead, jaw, and tongue.

6. Breathing

Do not change the breath.
Allow the body to breathe by itself.
Feel the natural rhythm of breathing in the belly, chest, or nostrils —
wherever it is easiest to sense.
When the mind wanders, always return to this simple bodily sensation.

7. Stability and Presence

The body is the **anchor of awareness.**
When the mind drifts into thoughts,
returning to bodily sensations grounds you again in the present.
A stable posture calms the mind,
and mindful embodiment lays the foundation for the deep silence of meditation.

Consistency in Practice

For effective progress, it is best to practice **every day** and establish a simple daily routine.
Even **five minutes a day** can be very beneficial.

Gradually increase the duration as you feel ready and inspired to continue.
Aim for **20–25 minutes**, and if you combine several practices,
you may extend to **30–40 minutes**.
If you skip a session from time to time, it is not a mistake and not a failure.
What matters most is that you **return** —
and integrate the practice as a natural part of your way of life.

Formal and Informal Meditation – A Simple Guidance

In this journey, you will meet two ways of practicing Presence:

Formal Meditation

This is the time you **set apart** each day for practice.
You sit (or stand, or lie) with intention —
a clear beginning, a clear duration, a single focus.
Here the mind learns stability, Presence and devotion.
This is your **anchor**.

Informal Meditation

This is Presence **within your daily life**:
walking, washing dishes, preparing food, speaking with others.
It turns ordinary moments into sacred moments.
Here the mind learns to stay open and aware while life is unfolding.
This is your **extension**.
Both forms support each other:
Formal practice **trains** the heart.
Informal practice **expresses** the heart.
One is the flame,
the other is the light it casts into the world.

Recognizing Consciousness – The First Moment of Awakening

Practice for (2-4 days)
Consciousness is like sunlight —
nothing illuminates it, for it is **the source of all light.**
You do not need to seek the light —
only notice that everything you see shines *from* it.
Thoughts and feelings are like clouds passing through the sky.
At times they veil the sun,
yet the sun never disappears.
The essence of meditation is to realize:
you are not the cloud —
but the light that shines behind it.
Sit or lie down comfortably.
Close your eyes and simply notice:
you are aware of being present.
Do not try to do anything.
Just observe that within you there is something
that perceives the body, the breath, the thoughts —
and yet itself never changes.
This **pure awareness** is what remains behind every experience.

Practice
Just observe.
Every perception — the breath, bodily sensations, thoughts — comes and goes.
For this practice you may Watch your breathing (do not control it in anyway)
See the breathing you breath in, and exhale and again
You can know you know the breathing happens because you are aware.
Remain with this simple recognition when you aware a perception that:
"I am aware that I am aware."
This is the foundation of meditation —

the recognition of **living presence.**

Body-Scanning Meditation – The Root of Awareness in the Body

Practice for (First time 2 weeks, every day, 30 minutes a day)
When awareness is already present, the next step is to connect with the body.

The body is the **gateway to presence**, and through attention we learn once more how to truly live within it.

Lie down or sit comfortably.

Begin by bringing attention to your toes,

and slowly move upward —

to the soles of the feet, the ankles, the shins, the knees,

the thighs, the pelvis, the abdomen, the chest,

the arms, shoulders, neck, face,

and finally the crown of the head.

At each point, simply notice what you feel —

warmth, tingling, emptiness, or perhaps nothing at all.

Whatever appears is perfectly fine.

If thoughts or emotions arise, do not reject them.

Just notice, perhaps labeling them gently as *"mental event"*

or *"thinking,"* and then softly return

to the part of the body where you left off.

Body scanning is not concentration, but **exploration** —

an experience of recognizing that every sensation and every thought

is perceivable, and that *you* are the one who perceives.

The Body as the Field of Awareness

Awareness is like the first light of dawn
gently sweeping across the earth.
It seeks nothing, changes nothing —
it simply illuminates what already is.

Where the light touches, everything becomes visible —
the dew, the flower, the stone.
Thus awareness moves through the body:
quietly, allowing, without judgment.
There is nothing to do —
only to let the light be present.
And as the body is seen, it naturally comes to rest.

Practice

Do this practice daily for about **20 minutes.**

(For this exercise, see "Practices in Depth" at the end of this book.)

The essence of the practice is not to achieve a perfect state of inner peace (although if it appears, we can calmly accept its presence) or to systematically observe every detail, but to maintain the **presence of awareness**. It is important to simply be **with whatever is happening**: feelings, tensions, discomfort, or joy.

If something strongly draws our attention away, we should not rush past it; instead, stay with it a little longer, and only then continue the practice. This process teaches us to be **fully present**, regardless of what feelings or bodily sensations arise. Over the years, this practice has brought me countless insights and a deep sense of inner freedom.

The Challenges of Inner Practice

When you begin to meditate, know that the path will not always feel peaceful.

Moments of discomfort, restlessness, and confusion will arise — not because something is wrong, but because what has long been suppressed begins to surface. Most human beings carry within them layers of unacknowledged thoughts, emotions, and forgotten tensions. Meditation simply brings light into these hidden rooms.

As awareness deepens, the mind starts to release what was once buried. This may appear as sadness, irritation, fear, or even physical unease. Yet these are not obstacles — they are signs of healing. Each sensation, each thought that arises, is asking to be seen and embraced in the light of consciousness.

If you approach these moments with acceptance, the heart gradually learns to remain open even amid discomfort. Over time, the mind grows accustomed to this openness and befriends what it once resisted. Thus, pain itself becomes part of awakening.

Do not turn away when practice feels unpleasant. Precisely then it is most fruitful to sit down and stay. If you practice only when it feels easy, the mind will never learn freedom. But if you stay present even when it feels difficult, awareness will grow stronger than the storm.

I too have walked through these passages — not lightly. There were times when silence seemed unbearable, when the inner world felt chaotic. Yet through patience and gentle persistence, the turbulence subsided, and clarity began to dawn.

Therefore, I encourage you: remain faithful to your practice.

Even in darkness, keep sitting.

Even in confusion, keep breathing.

For the light of God is not absent — it is simply purifying the places where you have not yet looked.

Listening to Sounds - Expanding Awareness

(10–25 minutes; for beginners, even 5 minutes is enough in the first day)
The next practice is **listening to sounds.**
Sit comfortably and allow sounds to reach you.
Do not seek them, do not analyze them.
There is nothing to find, avoid, or exclude.
Simply notice each sound — and notice also that you are **aware of hearing.**
Awareness recognizes the sound, yet is never caught in it.
If your attention drifts and you notice it,
there is no need for anger or guilt —

because the very act of noticing means that awareness is already present.

Begin by practicing with **pleasant sounds** for *three days* — birdsong, music, the sounds of nature.

Then move on to **neutral sounds** for *four days* — street noise, voices, wind.

Finally, practice with **unpleasant sounds** for t*hree days* — traffic, mechanical noise, disturbance.

After these in the future you can use it where ever you are, and for formal meditation you can use it with whatever sound is present, even silence is okay for it.

The aim is not to change the sounds,

but to recognize within every experience the same **silent awareness.**

The Mind Like a Still Lake

Awareness is like a calm lake.

Sounds create ripples on its surface,

yet the depths remain still.

When you hear a sound, simply observe

how it rises, moves, and fades.

The lake does not distinguish between the wind and the bird's song —

it reflects both equally.

Listen to the world in this same way:

without dividing good and bad,

allowing everything to return to the depth of silence.

Practice

From time to time, let go of listening to sounds altogether and simply *be.*

After a minute, return to listening.

Recognize that every sound — pleasant or unpleasant —

appears within the **space of awareness,**

and that **you yourself are that space.**

Walking Meditation – The Unity of Movement and Presence

(*About 15 minutes for 1-2 weeks*)
   Walking meditation helps you **sustain awareness while in motion.**
   Begin by standing still and feeling the ground beneath your feet.
   Then slowly start to move: **lifting, stepping, arriving.**
   Each movement is a moment within awareness.
   Notice the rhythm — as the body moves, consciousness accompanies it.
   Do not hurry.
   This is not about reaching a destination,
   but realizing that **each step is an arrival.**
   Walk in this way for 10–15 minutes daily, preferably in a quiet place,
   and feel how movement becomes the natural flow of presence itself.
   if you competently lost just be aware of that and you are already back in
awareness.

Open Awareness and Choiceless Awareness

(*Practice for 7 days, 15–25 minutes; 5 minutes is enough for beginners in the first
1-2 days*)
   When you have become familiar with the body and with sounds,
   you arrive at the state of **open awareness.**
   Here there is no longer any need to choose an object of focus:
   everything that arises becomes part of the practice.
   Consciousness is vast, receptive,
   and recognizes itself in all things.
   In time, attention fully relaxes —
   there is no longer observer and observed,
   only the flow of **conscious presence.**
   This is *choiceless awareness* — the deepest meditation,
   where there is nothing left to seek,
   for everything is already here.

The Mind Like the Boundless Sky

Consciousness is like an endless sky.
Thoughts, feelings, and memories are but clouds drifting across it.
The sky neither holds them back nor pushes them away.
The essence of meditation is not to disperse the clouds,
but to recognize the sky that remains untouched.
Freedom begins when you no longer identify with the clouds,
but recognize within yourself the sky itself.

Practice

Sit quietly and let everything be as it is —
thoughts, sensations, silence, noise — all of it.
Exclude nothing, grasp nothing.
Start where your mind IS, just let it be and see.
Here, consciousness awakens to itself
and realizes that **it is the very space in which all things exist.**
(For a detailed version of this exercise, see "Practices in Depth – Section C" at the end of this book.)
Meditation thus becomes the path of **awareness and recognition** —
the return of consciousness to itself.
Every form of practice leads here:
to the silence that is not empty,
but alive, loving, and aware.
From this silence arise true peace, compassion, and freedom.
Try to be this space, observe your consciousness your awareness.
You may be aware of sounds let be with them after that maybe a feelings catches your
awareness be with feelings, maybe after that a thought be with the thoughts
only necessary to be the space where everything happens in the eye of awareness.
if you competently lost just be aware of that and you are already back in awareness.

The Disciple of Awareness

A young disciple once asked the Master:

"Master, when will I become enlightened?"

The Master did not reply.
He simply lifted his gaze and pointed to a flower
that was just then opening its petals in the morning sun.
The disciple looked, but asked impatiently,

"What does this mean?"

The Master smiled.

"As long as you ask, you do not understand.
When you simply look, you already know."

The boy fell silent.
For a moment, the questions ceased.
There was no longer master and disciple —
only the flower and the silence.
In that stillness, knowledge was no longer in words,
but in the simple radiance of Being.
Then the Master spoke softly:

"The flower does not teach — yet it reveals everything.
You too are like this,
when you no longer try to become
what you already are."

Object Meditation – The Light of the World in the Mirror of Awareness

(Practice for 7 days, 10–15 minutes; for beginners, 5 minutes is enough in the first day)

In this meditation, attention does not turn inward but **outward** —
toward the world through which consciousness reflects itself.
The aim is not to analyze or name what you see or hear,
but to be **fully present** in the experience itself.
The outer world becomes the field of practice:
every sound, movement, light, and color
is an echo of awareness.
As Jesus said:

"He who has eyes to see, let him see."
For seeing itself is knowing.

The world is not outside of you —
the light you see is the reflection of consciousness.
When you gaze upon an object,
you are not merely seeing the object,
but the **light in which it appears.**
In contemplation, consciousness looks back upon itself —
like a mirror reflected in another mirror.
Then seeing becomes **prayer:**
the light of the world recognizes itself within you.

0. Setting up

Start every meditation where you attention is currently
after that you may start to feel your feet or where you sit on the pillow or chair
feel it completely as you sit on it after that go and feel your back and head and the full body.

1. Watching the Breath – The Gateway to Presence

Sit comfortably, with the back straight and the body relaxed.
Allow the breath to flow naturally.
Feel the air entering and leaving — like the rhythm of the world itself.
Remain with the breath for a few minutes,
so that the mind may settle and attention may find rest.

2. Opening Spacious Awareness

After observing the breath, let attention expand —
as when the horizon opens wide.
Do not look for anything specific to focus on;
simply sense that *everything* is included within this vastness.
This awareness does not concentrate on a single point —
it is like a boundless sky
in which everything can appear and pass away.
In this open space, consciousness rests —
not constricted, but breathing freely.
When you sense this spacious presence,
let awareness flow naturally into **outer perception.**

3. Opening to Outer Perception

Now gently allow your attention to move outward into space.
Notice the sounds around you — near and far.
Do not search for their source;
simply listen as if the world itself were breathing around you.
Observe the play of light and shadow,
the subtle movements.
Do not name anything, do not form thoughts.
Just allow everything to appear and dissolve
in the mirror of awareness.

4. Open Contemplation

Now open your eyes
   and let the whole field of sight fill your awareness.
   There is no need to focus on any single point —
   let the **entire space** become the object of meditation.
   Attention does not narrow; it widens.
   What is seen naturally becomes part of awareness itself.
   It is no longer *you* who looks at the world —
   the world is seeing itself through you.

Meditation on Feelings – Opening the Heart

(Practice for 7-10 days, 10–25 minutes; for beginners, 5 minutes is enough in the first day)
   When attention has become more stable, begin to observe **feelings**.
   Notice how they appear in the body: warmth, tightness, lightness, tension.
   Do not try to change them — simply acknowledge: *they are here.*
   As you observe, the emotion begins to move and slowly transforms.
   With stronger emotions, stay for a few moments with the sensations without sinking into them.
   Notice what other sensations they evoke — in the chest, throat, face, or abdomen.
   If you can, gently direct your attention to the most active area and ask yourself:
   "What is moving this feeling?"
   Perhaps avoidance, resistance, or a longing for safety.
   You don't need an answer — it is enough to recognize the movement itself.
   Sometimes the intensity of emotion may feel overwhelming.
   In such moments, remain with it briefly — simply acknowledging its presence —
   then gently shift your attention to another anchor, such as **listening**

meditation, breathing, or mindful walking.

Do not suppress or avoid the feeling; allow it to arise and stay with you for a while.

Let it unfold naturally in awareness, even as you rest your focus on the rhythm of sound, movement, or breath.

With more experience, even unpleasant emotions themselves can become **anchors of awareness —**

a living meditation where the feeling and the observer are not separate.

At other times, it may be wiser to take a short break:

do something that nourishes you — a walk, a gentle task, a moment of gratitude.

If the emotion reappears during the activity, simply notice it,

then return your attention to what you are doing.

At times it is helpful to examine sensations in detail.

For example, a frightening thought arises.

Notice which sensations accompany it:

— "A pulling on the left side of the forehead, a slight smoothness on the right."

Simply see what it is like: warm or cool, tight or pulsating.

Watch how sensations alternate like waves on the surface of the ocean.

Mindful attention is healing,

because whatever you behold with full awareness

slowly dissolves back —

not by suppression, but through gentle recognition.

Nothing needs to be changed — only **stayed with.**

When attention is loving and open, emotions loosen,

and the **silence of the heart** is revealed behind them.

The Waves of Feeling

Emotions are waves on the ocean of consciousness.

Sometimes stormy, sometimes barely noticeable.

If you resist them, they break you; if you drown in them, they sweep you away.

But if you observe them, you will see:

every wave returns to the sea from which it came.

Then you recognize: **you are the ocean** — not the wave, not the droplet,

but the depth that holds them all.

The peace of the heart is not the absence of feeling,

Practice

Begin by watching the **breath** for a few minutes,

then rest in **open awareness** and notice how everything unfolds within awareness.

After that, bring attention to areas where feelings often appear —

the forehead, face, shoulders, lower back, etc.

If an unpleasant feeling arises — for example, fear or sadness —

say quietly within: *"I am experiencing sadness."*

Remain with these areas for a few minutes,

then return to open awareness or to the breath.

Your attention is healing, because whatever you behold with full awareness

slowly returns to peace — through a gradual **befriending** of the experience.

(For a detailed version of this exercise, see "Practices in Depth – Section C" at the end of this book.)

Meditation on Thoughts - Recognizing the Play of the Mind

(Practice for 2 weeks, 10–25 minutes)

Sit quietly and allow thoughts to arise.

See them as images, words, or stories passing through the space of awareness.

Notice what feelings they evoke — joy, fear, desire, doubt.

Then recognize that thoughts are not truths, but passing phenomena.

Observe how they appear, remain for a moment, and fade away.

Notice also the space between them — the clear, open field of awareness itself.

When a new thought arises, allow it too — just as it is.

Simply observe the play of the mind, while resting as the still awareness that never moves.

Thoughts can appear on **three levels**:

as **words** — inner voices that arise in your own tone or the voices of others;

as **images** — mental pictures, scenes, or visions;

and as **sensations** — bodily feelings that the mind projects like a *4D movie*, creating the sense of physical experience.

Try this experiment:

Sit quietly and follow your breathing for 5–10 inhalations and exhalations.

Then imagine walking barefoot through a dark room at night —

and suddenly stepping on something sharp, like the edge of a cube.

Or imagine accidentally hitting your little toe on the corner of a table.

Or, if you prefer, picture yourself in a thicket where a large thorn pierces the palm of your hand, about three to five centimeters deep.

You may feel a brief discomfort — but nothing real has happened.

You simply **imagined** a situation that produced sensations and reactions in the body.

This shows that thoughts and images are *not facts* but *mental projections* — assumptions about what *might* happen or how you *might* react.

They are not reality itself.

Even strong sensations born from imagination dissolve once you see them for what they are:

temporary appearances within awareness.

The thoughts are like **clouds upon the face of the sky.**

Some drift slowly, others rush in storms — yet none remain forever.

If you try to drive them away, they only grow stronger;

if you follow them, you lose sight of the sky.

Simply observe them as they come and go,

while the sky itself remains unchanged.

Consciousness is the sky — vast, untouched, bathed in light.

When you recognize this, there is no need to quiet the mind —

the clouds **dissolve on their own** in the nature of the light.

Practice

Sit comfortably and allow your body to rest.

Take a few deep, natural breaths.

Do not control the breathing — let it happen by itself.

Feel the air entering... and leaving.

The chest rising... and falling.

Breathing happens on its own — you simply observe.

This **attention** is the gateway to awareness.

Now, turn your awareness inward for a moment.

Notice that **you are aware.**

Not of something — but simply aware of being aware.

This awareness is what sees everything.

Here there is no effort, no goal — only presence.

Rest for a few breaths in this open space.

Then let whatever wants to appear, appear.

Perhaps a thought, an image, a sentence.

It's fine if it comes — it may move freely in the field of awareness.

Simply notice: *"thought."*

You don't need to finish it or push it away.

Just see it arise, then fade —

like a cloud drifting across the sky.

Now let your attention expand again.

Notice that there is not only the thought —

but also the **space behind it** in which it arose.

That space *is* awareness itself.

It does not move or change;

it simply sees what comes and goes.

Stay in this open awareness for a few moments.

Another thought may appear — a plan, a memory, a phrase.

Once again, simply notice: *"thought."*

And the moment you recognize it,

you have already returned to the spacious field of awareness.
Do not try to make thoughts disappear.
The goal is not emptiness,
but to see that awareness perceives while everything changes.
Both silence and thought are parts of the same awareness.
Now observe:
before every thought, there is a brief moment of silence.
And after every thought — that same silence remains.
This silence is not empty, but awake.
In it, awareness rests.
Let your attention shift naturally —
sometimes resting in a thought,
sometimes expanding again into open awareness.
There is nothing to do, nothing to control.
Awareness naturally returns to itself.
Slowly you will begin to see that thoughts are not enemies.
They do not disturb you — only when you believe them.
But when you see them as waves on the surface of the ocean,
you are already in the depth where peace resides.
Stay like this for a few breaths:
mind and thought existing together,
like sky and clouds — never truly separate.
Inhale and feel: *"I am here."*
Exhale and feel: *"I allow it to be."*
And when you open your eyes,
remember — thoughts will appear throughout the day.
But now you know:
you don't have to follow each one.
Simply notice them arising in the space of awareness —
and let that space remain always **wider** than the thoughts themselves.
This recognition is the **taming of the mind** —
not through struggle, but through **seeing.**

The Dance of Emotions and Thoughts

Every emotion that arises within us is a gateway to the deeper layers of consciousness. When we feel anxiety, sadness, or longing, these waves of emotion do not exist in isolation—they give rise to thoughts as well. A compulsion to avoid, a fear, or an inner judgment often manifests not only as a feeling but also as a thought: "I am not enough," "I must avoid this," "What if...?" In this way, emotion creates thought, as if the soul were whispering a message, which the mind transforms into images, words, and stories.

At the same time, thoughts also influence our emotional state. A recurring fear, a pessimistic imagination, or an inner narrative born of guilt can summon waves of worry, sadness, or restlessness. Thoughts and emotions thus engage in a continuous dance with one another: each gives rise to the other, and both are fleeting phenomena, revealing only the momentary states of consciousness rather than absolute reality.

Inner attention teaches us not to identify with either the emotion or the thought. When we are simply present with the arising feeling, observing the waves that emerge in the body, and at the same time notice the thoughts—without judgment, without following them—we gradually begin to understand the subtle interplay between them. We learn that thoughts and emotions are transient phenomena, and they only yield to the inner silence when we do not identify with them, but allow the observing consciousness— the inner light—to awaken, which is always present.

In this attentive presence, thoughts and emotions no longer dominate us; they serve as guides, revealing where we dwell in the present moment, where suppressed feelings are hidden, and where the inner light calls us to reconnect with ourselves.

And yet, we need not avoid them so much; if we recognize that a passing thought is merely a sign of fleeting bad mood or a sense of abandonment, it is like switching sunglasses: the colors and shapes of the world shift through them, but it is not the reality itself. Or like a cloud casting a shadow— the thought colors and shapes our perception, but it is not identical with reality. Just as the weather changes—sunny, clear, overcast, or stormy with lightning—so too do thoughts and feelings come and go; transient phenomena that do not define us. The sky itself, which holds all this, remains unchanged; in the same way, consciousness—your true Self—is like the sky, the silent presence that stands above every wave, always here, always receptive.

Emotions and thoughts are often difficult to handle, generating anxiety, depression, or inner tension. In meditation, the goal is not merely to allow them, but to truly be **present with these experiences**. When we observe with attention and acceptance:

- Let the feelings arise and pass according to their own nature.
- The reflex to avoid and the inner resistance diminish.
- It becomes easier to be with our emotions, even when they are strong.

Afterwards, observation and, if helpful, labeling can follow, which allows us to see the **transient nature** of emotions and thoughts. We can notice that they are merely **mental movies**, not our reality.

From my own experience, this state brings a much greater sense of freedom. If the emotions return, they no longer appear as enemies; instead, **divine acceptance** supports our presence with them. In this way, they dissolve in the light of awareness, and the presence of the soul provides a supportive anchor.

Since I have been practicing in this way—allowing everything to simply be present and observing it with curious acceptance—I have found it much easier to make friends with my sensations and thoughts. I recognize that they are not facts, not truths, and not who I am.

10

Meditation in Daily Life – Living in the Presence of the Soul

Meditation is not merely the art of sitting on a cushion. True practice begins the moment you rise from it. As long as meditation is confined to quiet moments, it has not yet become life itself.

But when you recall awareness again and again throughout the day, then practice *becomes* life.

Jesus lived this way — in Presence, in the Spirit of the moment.

He did not only pray — He *was* the prayer.

Learn to bring meditation into the movements of everyday life.

You do not always need to sit down.

It is enough to **remember.**

When you walk, say silently:

"Now I am practicing walking meditation."

Feel the rhythm of your steps,

the ground supporting you,

and let the body's movement gently return you to the present.

When you hear a sound, simply notice:

"Now I am practicing sound meditation."

Let the sounds come and go like waves upon the shore.

When you feel something — joy, anger, fear, or love — say to yourself:
"Now I am practicing emotion meditation."
Watch the feeling arise, change, and slowly dissolve like a cloud in the sky.
Do not fight it. Simply witness what is.
When a thought appears, let it pass as you notice:
"Now I am practicing thought meditation."
Thoughts are not enemies but teachers —
they show you where you have drifted away from Presence.
You can move freely between these forms throughout the day.
Meditation is not a rigid system but a **living relationship with the Spirit.**
Only one thing is needed: to remember again and again.
Remember Presence — and you are already where Heaven begins: *within you.*

The Practice of Conscious Response — Meeting Unpleasant Sensations

The true meaning of meditation is revealed when peace is disturbed.

When tension, anxiety, pain, or an unpleasant thought arises — do not escape it.

Use it as meditation.

This is the moment when practice comes alive.

As soon as you notice discomfort, pause,

and call upon this brief **mindful response practice:**

1. **Recognize the thought.**
2. See that it has appeared — and watch it fade.
3. Remind yourself: *"This is only a thought, not reality."*
4. **Turn toward the emotion.**
5. Name it if you can: *sadness, anger, fear, anxiety, resistance, avoidance.*
6. Do not judge it — simply acknowledge: *"This is what is present now."*
7. **Observe the bodily sensation.**
8. Where do you feel it? Chest, stomach, throat, forehead?
9. What is its quality? Pressure, warmth, tingling, emptiness?
10. Do not suppress or change it — just let it be,

11. and watch with gentle curiosity as it moves or transforms.
12. **Breathe consciously.**
13. Take six slow, deep breaths.
14. With each exhale, allow more space to open within you.
15. **Return to present reality.**
16. Feel your body as it is now — your feet on the ground,
17. the air on your skin, the world around you.
18. Let awareness expand to include everything —
19. thoughts, sounds, sensations — without excluding anything.

Then continue what you were doing —
or choose another action that uplifts you or serves the world.
The key is this: **let awareness lead, not emotion.**
In this way, every difficulty becomes a teacher of the Soul.
When unpleasant thoughts or sensations arise,
you stand before a sacred choice.
One path is to resist, suppress, or escape —
which only strengthens what you fight.
Each new tension in the body is born from the attempt to avoid another.
But even if resistance arises, in the light of awareness you can choose differently —
to observe with acceptance, seeing things as they are.
Recognize thoughts and sensations as they appear,
and gently apply the mindful response practice.
Begin with pleasant sensations and easy situations.
As you grow in steadiness, move gradually toward more difficult ones.
It is equally valuable to bring awareness to what is joyful —
to know your patterns and use that knowledge later for transformation.
When walking, savor the sound of the forest;
when showering, feel the warm water as a living meditation.
Every moment can reveal the presence of the Spirit.

Epictetus taught:

"It's not what happens to you, but how you react to it that matters."

The Meditation of the Witness – The Practice of Labeling
There is a simple yet powerful practice
that helps you remain awake and present with any experience: **labeling meditation.**
It teaches you to recognize what is happening within you
without getting lost in it or fighting against it.
Sit or stand comfortably.
Let your attention flow naturally — there is nothing to search for or achieve.
Simply **observe.**
When something appears, gently name what you perceive:

- If a thought arises: *"thought."*
- If an emotion arises: *"emotion"* — such as *anger, sadness, joy, fear.*
- If a desire appears: *"desire."*
- If an impulse to avoid arises: *"avoidance."*
- If you sense the body: *"sensation"* — *warmth, pressure, tingling.*

Do not try to control or change anything.
Just recognize what is present and let it pass,
like a cloud drifting through the sky.
Labeling is not analysis — it is pure recognition.
The moment you name what you experience,
awareness awakens and the experience loses its power over you.
In the light of awareness, every phenomenon reveals itself
and returns to the silence from which it came.
You can practice this anytime —
while sitting, walking, waiting, or after a conversation in a few quiet breaths.
The more you practice, the more you realize:

you are not the thought or the emotion —
you are the one who is **aware** of them.
When this recognition is present in every movement,
meditation is no longer a practice —
it becomes a way of life,
the Soul's living breath in the world.

11

The Art of Allowing

Acceptance is not passive resignation, but the deepest form of conscious presence.

When we accept something — a thought, an emotion, a bodily sensation, or an external event — we simply observe it without rejecting it or clinging to it.

We let it be as it is, without acting upon it.

Just see as it appears, existing for a bit then, cease to exists by it self, it may come back again or not, its not important just the act of seeing it and being with it until it moves away like a cloud.

This simple yet powerful gesture dissolves suffering at its root.

When we resist what is, we create inner tension.

The mind begins to fight reality, and this struggle gives rise to stress, anxiety, and depressive patterns of thought and emotion.

The more we try to avoid unpleasant feelings, the deeper they take root within us.

Attention and acceptance gradually dissolve them — not because we make it our goal, but because space naturally opens for transformation.

True acceptance seeks to change nothing.

It simply remains present with whatever is.

If you feel discomfort, notice exactly where and how it manifests in the body.

If a thought arises, recognize it as just that — a thought, not reality itself.

If you feel an impulse to avoid, distract, or fight, notice that too.

You need not follow anything.

Simply watch as everything appears and fades within the vast field of awareness.

This is also the remedy for sleeplessness.

When we *try* to fall asleep, sleep drifts further away.

But if we allow wakefulness to be, and observe the contact of the bed, the movement of the breath, the weight of the body on the mattress — tension begins to dissolve.

No goal is needed.

In acceptance, peace arises naturally.

This attitude is not merely a psychological technique, but the most direct path to divine grace.

Acceptance is the highest divine principle, for it mirrors how divine consciousness embraces all things without judgment.

When we accept, we participate in this grace.

The act of acceptance is the movement of the Spirit itself:

God says "yes" to life — and within us, that *yes* is born as well.

Epictetus taught:

"It is not things themselves that disturb us, but the way we judge them."

"Do not wish that things happen as you want them to; wish instead that they happen as they do — and you will be happy."

"Do not wish that events happen as you desire, but desire that they happen as they do, and all will go well."

The wise understand that the events of life cannot be controlled — but our attitude toward them can. Acceptance does not mean liking what happens, but refusing to close the heart against it. As long as we fight reality, we live in bondage.

When we open to it, we return to freedom.

The Boundaries of Influence and Control

Human freedom does not lie in controlling everything, but in recognizing what we truly can and cannot influence.

We cannot control the weather, other people's behavior, the events of the past, or every function of the body.

But we can direct our **attention**, our **attitude**, and the way we **respond** to the present moment.

Stoic wisdom expresses it simply:

> *"Some things are within our power, and others are not.*
> *The wise person distinguishes between the two."*

When we accept what cannot be changed and focus our full awareness on what can — the clarity of our mind, the present moment, the openness of our heart —

we return to inner peace.

Resistance turns into cooperation, struggle into trust, tension into stillness.

Thus, acceptance is not weakness, but the manifestation of divine strength within us.

The one who accepts does not give up — they surrender to what truly *is.*

And in this surrender, divine presence dawns like the light of morning after a storm.

Hermetic Understanding of Acceptance

According to the Hermetic teachings, the world is not a chain of random events,

but the movement of the *Logos* — the Divine Mind — within itself.

Those who recognize this no longer live on the surface of events, but within the divine Current that flows beneath them.

The Hermetic sages taught that humanity's task is not to resist the flow of life,

but to understand it and move in harmony with it.

Every experience, joy, and challenge is an expression of the Cosmic Law — the journey of the Soul returning to the One.

> *"Let your will be one with the Divine Will, and you will no longer be a slave of fate."*
>
> *"All things unfold as the One wills them; man's task is to understand and to flow with that will."*

Resistance always strengthens duality — the conflict between good and bad, right and wrong —

while acceptance restores us to wholeness,

where everything arises from the One.

The events of the world are not enemies but teachers.

Pain, loss, and sudden change are all calls of the Soul to know itself more deeply.

Through the eyes of the Hermetic master, nothing happens by chance:

every movement is the rhythm of the Divine Spirit through which creation learns to behold itself.

Whoever realizes this enters the divine Current through acceptance —

into the peace where one no longer asks, "Why did this happen?"

but understands that everything happens exactly as the Soul requires.

This acceptance is the highest form of conscious presence.

It is not rejection of the world, but vision of the Whole —

the recognition that everything is in its rightful place.

When a person lives this way, the human will and the Divine Will become one,

and the Soul ceases to be the prisoner of fate,

becoming instead the bearer of divine Order in the world.

The Dynamics of Procrastination and the Release of Self-Sabotage

We often feel that we "cannot" start something. Behind procrastination, however, there is not laziness, but a natural fear of suffering. We imagine in advance that the task will be difficult, uncomfortable, or painful. This creates resistance even before we begin.

Yet when we pause and recognize that much of this perceived difficulty is **merely the product of our own judgment and inner resistance**, a new possibility arises: we can allow the task to be as it is and simply begin.

This conscious choice—not fighting against the imagined difficulty, but accepting reality and taking action—**reduces self-sabotage** and frees the energy within us to act. The more we allow ourselves to simply carry out the task, the weaker procrastination becomes, and the space once occupied by resistance is gradually replaced by openness and acceptance.

The Nature of Attachment and Letting Go

Attachment arises when we try to make permanent that which is, by its very nature, impermanent. This could be a relationship, food, a home, silence, peace, or life itself – nothing remains the same forever. When we believe something is permanent and do everything to keep it unchanged, we create inner tension and suffering. Attachment becomes an emotional bond: it chains us, limits us, and prevents us from fully experiencing the present moment.

The key to releasing attachment lies in acceptance and awareness. By observing our desires, fears, and emotional reactions, we learn to recognize the signs of attachment. It is not about suppressing our desires or eliminating our feelings, but about learning to allow things to be as they are, and to let change happen – even when it feels emotionally challenging.

Practical Tips for Relationships

Offer your full presence and attention to yourself and your partner. Do not try to manipulate or control the other to keep the relationship – this only creates falsehoods and fractures in the soul. This can create inner conflict and diminish the freedom of both partners. If your partner chooses to leave, simply observe and accept their decision. This is genuine love, which brings freedom and trust to both individuals.

Take a gentle look at your situation: notice how much time, attention, and care you have shared with your partner. If obstacles such as work, stress, or inner fears have arisen, simply observe the ways these may have influenced your presence and intimacy with the partner. At the same time, pay attention to your partner's patterns: how they relate to their own desires, fears, habits, and past experiences. There is no blame here; sometimes mental and emotional patterns simply do not align, which can create tension or a sense of distance.

Self-Reflection Practice:

- What are we feeling right now? Fear, sadness, disappointment?
- What are we expecting from our partner that causes suffering?
- Which past experiences are being triggered in this moment?
- How does the partner's behavior reflect our own patterns?
- What types of people do we attract, and what can we learn from our past relational patterns?

If a new relationship enters your life, allow it to unfold on new foundations, with different mental patterns and fresh possibilities. This is not only about the partner but also about your own patterns, self-knowledge, and the experience of inner freedom.

In General: In any form of attachment – whether to objects, experiences, or personal comfort – the essential practice is to fully experience each moment as it is, then allow it to pass. Acceptance and presence are not passivity; they are the experience of freedom. The mind releases the chains of illusion and is able to embrace change without being harmed.

The practice, then, is to observe, acknowledge, and fully live what is, and to allow things to come and go as they naturally do. This is true inner freedom – the state of love and acceptance – which can be present in every moment, if we dare to let reality be as it is.

Prayer for Acceptance

Grant me, O Lord,

the wisdom to discern what I can change and what I cannot.

Grant me the strength to change what I can,

and the peace to accept what I cannot.

Teach me to trust that everything unfolds as it must,

and that the current of my life rests safely in Your hands.

The Highest Form of Love: Unconditional Acceptance and Forgiveness

Love, in its purest form, is not desire, attachment, or even affection — it is the radiant recognition of the divine in all beings.

When love is free from condition, it becomes the mirror of the Divine Heart itself.

Unconditional acceptance is the highest expression of this love, for it embraces everything — joy and sorrow, virtue and error, light and shadow — as parts of one divine movement.

Forgiveness is its natural fragrance.

To forgive is not to forget or to excuse, but to release the judgment that separates.

Through forgiveness, we remember that nothing real can be lost, and nothing unreal can harm the soul.

What we forgive in others, we heal within ourselves.

This is the supreme act of divine participation — to love without demand, to forgive without expectation, and to see the face of God in every being.

In such love, resistance dissolves, and we return to the unity from which all creation flows.

This is the love that the Hermetic sages called *the Fire of the One*, and which Christ revealed as the eternal commandment:

"Love one another as I have loved you."

When this love is born in the heart, acceptance is no longer a practice — it is our natural state.

Forgiveness becomes effortless, for there is no longer anyone left to forgive, only the One through whom all beings move and have their being.

12

Childlike Presence

A child never wonders whether they are happy — they simply are.
They do not plan, compare, or judge.
Every moment is new; every touch, sound, and color a discovery.
For them, the world is not made of concepts, but of living light.
The child's consciousness does not try to control anything,
because it has not yet separated itself from what it perceives.
This is the natural state — **pure presence.**
A child does not try *to be present* — they *are* presence itself.
Their attention is not something they direct;
it flows freely, like a clear mountain stream.
And because no thought stands between them and the world,
they see reality in the fresh light of God.

> *"Unless you become like little children, you will never enter the Kingdom of Heaven."*
> — Matthew 18:3

The words of Jesus were not moral teachings, but truths of consciousness.
The Kingdom of Heaven is not a place in space,
but a state of awareness — the point where the observer and the observed
are one,

where there is no "I" that seeks, only Life beholding itself.

The Memory of Childlike Moments

As a child, you may have felt that same pure, unexplainable peace —
a moment when everything inside you grew still,
and all became vivid, radiant, alive.
When you simply looked — at a tree, an insect, or light dancing on water
—

and there was no thought, only presence.
Nothing was missing, nothing needed to be reached —
yet *you were completely there.*
A pause in time, where consciousness did nothing but *be.*
Many adults rediscover this presence in nature —
when they stop, fall silent, and something within them begins to observe.
It is the same source, the same purity — now joined with awareness.
These moments are not new experiences,
but remembrances of something that has never truly left.

The Challenge of Modern Childhood

Children today grow up surrounded by screens.
Their attention is captured early by rapidly changing images, sounds, and
impulses.
They have fewer and fewer moments simply *to be* —
to pause, to look, and to feel the quiet radiance that existence itself gives.
Many may never experience that natural attention
which earlier generations knew instinctively.
They touch that presence only when the screens go dark —
when their awareness returns to reality:
to the sound of the wind, the light, or another person's gaze.
Constant digital noise separates them from the natural silence,
and thus from their true selves.
The effects are already visible: restlessness, distraction, anxiety, and an
inner emptiness.

But the essence is not lost —
it only waits to be recognized and remembered within us.

The Second Innocence
The spiritual path is not a return to childhood,
but the *rebirth of childlike awareness within the adult mind.*
The mystic is not childish, but **consciously innocent.**
In contemplative attention, the purity that was once spontaneous
opens again — now mature, understood, and turned toward God.
This is what Teresa of Ávila called
"the soul's return to the inner castle."
Conscious childlikeness is the deepest form of wisdom:
when presence is awake, the heart sees again.

Contemplative Question

"Do you remember what it was like as a child —
when you didn't analyze or think,
but simply lived what was happening?"

Imagine your life, from your very first memories until this very moment.
What has been there all along — unchanging, linking every experience
together?
Not the circumstances — they have constantly shifted.
Not the people — they have come and gone.
Not even the body, which has transformed day by day.
Not the thoughts or emotions — they too have faded and been replaced.
What remains is *that which perceives it all.*
That which is unchanging amidst all change.
That is **You** — the Awareness that sees everything.

13

Transforming Words and Thoughts – The Language of Experiential Awareness

Whit hen we say, "I am sad," "I am afraid," or "I am angry," there is a deep error hidden within those words.

Because in saying them, we identify ourselves with what merely passes through us.

We mistake a fleeting inner wave for our very self.

Yet you are not sadness — you are the awareness that sees sadness.

You are not fear — you are the one who perceives that fear has appeared within the field of consciousness.

This difference seems small, yet inwardly it is revolutionary.

A single word separates suffering from freedom:

the difference between *"I am"* and *"I am experiencing."*

When you say:

– "I am experiencing sadness right now."

– "I feel fear in my chest."

– "The energy of anger is present."

you no longer identify with it, but consciously remain present to what is happening.

You are no longer a plaything of emotion, but hold it within the vast space of awareness.

This language does not alienate — it liberates.

It allows feelings to come and go,

while *you* remain — the silent Witness, the Christ Consciousness.

When you speak in this way, you are retraining the mind to recognize reality.

You show it that there is nothing to fight, suppress, or fix —

only to observe, to be present, and to lovingly allow all to be.

From this point, even pain transforms:

suffering becomes *witnessing*,

and *my problem* becomes *a divine flow*.

And slowly you realize:

you no longer need to say, "I am sad,"

because you know — sadness is only a guest in your home.

You are the Home itself.

14

The Practice of the Contemplative Life – How to Walk in the Spirit

The Contemplative Life as Living Prayer

The contemplative life is not an isolated practice, not a separate period of meditation during the day, but a way of being.

It is a presence that consecrates every moment.

As the ancient fathers said: *"Pray without ceasing."*

But what does this mean?

It is not to repeat words endlessly, but to place consciousness again and again in the presence of God.

The contemplative life is nothing other than the silent attention of the heart, open to the movement of the Spirit — like a window left ajar, through which the eternal light fills the room.

This living prayer is neither noisy nor spectacular.

Outwardly, a person may simply walk, listen, go about their tasks.

But within, a temple is being built where humanity and divinity lean into one another.

Presence is the altar where Christ takes form in every moment, if we are attentive.

For every moment is sacred when the awareness of God shines within it.

The saints were not holy because of what they did, but because of *how* they were present.

Thus, the contemplative life transforms every situation into an opportunity for prayer:

washing dishes, walking, working, speaking — all become chances for the heart's attention to rest in God.

Silence here is not the absence of sound, but the awakened stillness of the spirit that no longer strives — it simply *is.*

In this presence, it is no longer the self who prays, but God praying within us to Himself.

Practical Instruction – Presence in Daily Life

Choose a simple activity in your day — walking, washing dishes, dressing, or washing your hands.

As you do it, bring your full attention here: feel the movements, the sensations in your body, the sounds.

If your mind wanders, gently return.

Do not judge — just observe.

This mindful presence is the silent prayer of the heart.

The Body as Sacred Instrument – The Prayer of Movement

Many separate the spiritual from the physical, as if the body were an obstacle.

Yet the body is the vessel of the Spirit, and every movement can become prayer when done consciously.

The body is not the prison of the spirit, but its sanctuary.

Every step, every gesture, every breath can carry presence — if we no longer rush ahead of it.

When one walks with awareness, each step becomes sacred.

It is as if the earth beneath turns into holy ground, sanctified by consciousness itself.

It is not the movement that is special, but the awareness that fills it.

One who walks this way is not merely going somewhere — they are coming home with every step.

Contemplative walking is simple: move slowly, with awareness, feeling the ground, the muscles, the breath.

There is nothing to achieve — only to be present.

The same applies to eating.

Every bite can be an eucharistic act — gratitude, receiving, life.

Bread is not just nourishment — it is a symbol of Christ.

Water is not just fluid — it is the flow of the Spirit.

The body is not a distraction, but a gateway through which God enters.

When we treat the body as sacred, we realize that God dwells not only in temples — but within us.

Practical Instruction – Contemplative Walking

Stand still, then begin to walk slowly.

Notice how the foot lifts, moves forward, and touches the ground.

Step by step, keep returning your attention to the physical experience of movement.

Breathe naturally.

If thoughts arise, notice them and return to the sensation of walking.

This is prayer in motion.

Hearing as Divine Reception

Few practices sanctify us as deeply as attentive listening — not only to human words but to the sounds of life itself.

Birdsong, the wind, breathing, another's sigh — all are languages of God.

One who learns to listen does not focus on content, but on the silence behind the sound.

And in that silence, God speaks.

Silence is not emptiness, but fullness — the womb from which all sound is born and to which it returns.

In this practice, we simply receive sounds without judgment, labeling, or selection.

We do not seek meaning — we allow them to be.

Thus, the world ceases to be an object and becomes presence.

And gradually we see: the world is not *speaking to us* — it is *speaking within us.*

The bird does not sing *for* us — Being sings to itself.

We are merely the silent witnesses.

Contemplative listening is not passive; it is deeply receptive.

This receptivity is not curious but reverent; not analytical but open.

God reveals Himself in such attention — not as the meaning of words, but as the soft murmur of the Spirit that pervades all creation.

Practical Instruction – Listening to Sounds

Sit quietly and bring your attention to the sounds reaching you.

Do not search for them — let them come.

Observe them without naming.

Just listen.

If attention wanders, return to the next sound.

Sense the silence between them — and how the presence of God unfolds from that silence.

The Breath

Breathing is our first and last act in this world.

It is always with us — yet rarely do we notice it.

In the contemplative life, breathing is not a mere bodily function, but prayer: the breath of the Spirit within us.

When we attend to the breath, we not only calm the mind but commune with the One who gave us life.

Breath is relationship — the ongoing union of God and humanity.

A simple practice: sit quietly, observing each inhalation and exhalation without trying to change it.

Every breath is God's whisper: *"I am here."*

And we respond: *"And I am here."*

A silent dialogue unfolds — wordless yet alive.

In this prayer, the body and Spirit breathe together.

Breathing is not merely an aid to prayer — it *is* the prayer.

Whoever lives in this awareness discovers that every moment is a new opportunity to enter the Present and meet the Living One.

The air we breathe is the same breath that, in the beginning, gave life to humankind.

That breath is still within us.

With every inhalation, creation happens anew.

Practical Instruction – Awareness of Breath

Sit comfortably with a straight back.

Bring attention to your breath.

Notice where you feel it most — at the nostrils, the chest, or the belly.

Do not control it — simply follow it.

If the mind drifts, notice it and gently return to the breath.

Stay for a few minutes — this is the prayer of presence.

Observing Thoughts and Feelings

The mind is not empty.

Thoughts, emotions, and images arise and pass away.

But these are not the problem — identification is.

One of the holiest contemplative practices is learning to observe what happens within without interference.

This requires deep humility: the willingness to release the desire to control, understand, or manipulate.

Simply to see, as clouds drift across the sky — and to know: *we are the sky*.

Thoughts may come. Emotions may rise.

But the contemplative does not become what they see — they remain present.

This presence is gentle yet powerful, like a mother watching her child play — not intervening, but fully there in love.

God looks upon the world within us in the same way — and we can learn to look upon ourselves with that same gaze.

This attention heals, for it is filled with love and demands no change — and through that very love, all is transformed.

Practical Instruction – Watching Thoughts

Sit quietly and turn your awareness inward.

Observe the thoughts, images, and emotions that arise.

Do not try to eliminate or analyze them — simply watch.

Imagine them as clouds drifting across the sky.

You are not the thought — you are the one who sees.

If you get lost in a thought, return to your breath or body sensations.

Form as the Reflection of the Divine

Ultimately, every form we perceive is an opportunity — a reflection of God's presence.

A tree, a human face, a stone — none are *just* something, but unique expressions of Being.

The contemplative mind does not categorize, but receives.

And in that receptivity, form becomes transparent — revealing the Invisible behind it.

The world is not a collection of separate objects, but a tapestry of sacred icons through which God reveals Himself.

This is not imagination, but vision.

Not mystical haze, but purity of heart.

As the Gospel says: *"Blessed are the pure in heart, for they shall see God."*

In the contemplative life, this seeing is not a special experience but a natural state.

The world is no longer an obstacle, but a window.

Form no longer distracts from presence — it deepens it.

For behind every form stands the Formless: the Being present in all.

Practical Instruction – Seeing Meditation

Choose a simple object: a candle, a leaf, a stone, or a face.

Gaze at it attentively, without naming or creating stories about it.

Observe its shape, color, texture.

Sense how something more — a divine presence — shines through it.

When the mind wanders, return to the object.

Stay open to the presence behind the form.

The Natural Goodness of Consciousness and the Human Heart

At the core of every human being lies a simple yet profound truth: we do not wish to suffer, and we long to be happy.

This is not weakness but the imprint of the divine image within us.

The movement away from pain and toward joy, peace, and love is the soul's turning toward its Source.

This is a drop of the divine nature — the fundamental goodness of the heart.

Just as awareness dwells in every human, so does this goodness.

It need not be earned or attained — only recognized.

Like a light at the bottom of a lake, covered by silt and waves — yet the light has never gone out.

Within every mind there is this witnessing presence — non-judging, non-reactive, simply seeing.

It is the same light that shone in the gaze of Jesus.

This seeing is the gaze of Christ within us.

When we are present, attentive, and no longer flee from the moment, it is the Christ-consciousness acting in us.

Such awareness is not passive — it is filled with love.

Therefore, the contemplative practice is not a special skill but a return to who we have always been: the pure-hearted seers.

Loving-Kindness – The Practice of the Heart

One of the deepest fruits of the contemplative life is the flowering of loving-kindness.

Loving-kindness is the heart's response to the world's suffering:

"I see you. I am with you. May you be at peace."

This disposition extends not only to others — but also to ourselves.

See the related meditation in the chapter 22 **"Love and Compassion as the Foundation of Consciousness,"** in the section **"The Expansion of Love."**

15

Spacious Awareness – Being Present in God

Consciousness Is Not a Tool, but Divine Presence
Most people think of consciousness as something to *use*: *I focus, I pay attention, I am present.*

Yet the deeper truth of the contemplative path is that consciousness is not a tool, but a source.

It is not something we *do* — it is what we *are*.

This vast, clear awareness — within which thoughts, feelings, and experiences arise — is God within us.

This awareness does not judge, reject, or desire anything.

It simply *is*.

It is as spacious as the sky.

Every movement, every thought, every sound arises and passes away within this space —

appearing, lingering, dissolving, perhaps returning again —

yet the space itself never changes.

That space *is* presence.

And that presence is not some force *behind* the "self" — it is the true Self.

"I Am That I Am."

The Realization of the "I Am"

Jesus said, *"Before Abraham was, I am."*

This was not a personal statement but a declaration of awareness.

The **"I Am"** is not the historical life, nor the ego —

it is the unchanging, ever-present consciousness that witnesses every experience.

When we rest in awareness, we do not withdraw from the world — our vision transforms.

We no longer see *things* — we see *Being* behind all things.

Questions fade, and a silent knowing arises.

The realization of the "I Am" is not a thought but a direct experience —

a homecoming into the Self who, in truth, is none other than God.

The Space Between Thoughts – The Presence of God

Many believe that silence comes when thoughts disappear.

But silence is always here — between thoughts, beneath them, behind them.

This silence is not emptiness, but the field of pure awareness.

Within this space, God does not "appear" — He is already present,

waiting only for us to rest in Him.

When we learn not to cling to any thought, but to let them come and go freely,

the space of awareness expands.

This space *is* peace.

Here there is nothing to prove, nothing to control.

Here everything happens — and yet, nothing happens.

This is where the Spirit breathes,

and where we recognize: *This is who I am.*

This "nothingness" is the greatest fullness — for it holds not something, but *everything.*

Contemplative Rest

Spacious awareness cannot be created — only discovered.

Every contemplative practice ultimately leads us back to this space.

We are not focusing on experiences, but on the space in which experience unfolds.

This space *is* God.

And in this recognition, the search ends — for everything has arrived.

Thus, the deepest practice is the practice of *non-doing*:

to sit, to be, to strive for nothing, to fix nothing, to reach for nothing — simply to allow yourself to be *as you are.*

Here, it is no longer *I* who watch God —

but *God being present as me.*

This is not arrogance, but humble awakening —

a realization that God already exists within us, as awareness itself.

Practical Instruction – Awareness as the Experience of God

(20–25 minutes per day; begin with 10–15 minutes if you are new.

This form of meditation is best practiced once you are familiar with breathing, sound, thought, and feeling awareness.)

Sit comfortably, allowing your body to be relaxed.

Bring your attention to *space*, not to *things.*

Do not concentrate — rather, rest into what is already here.

Begin wherever your awareness naturally is.

Notice sounds, sensations, thoughts — but cling to none.

When you realize you've drifted into something, gently return to the sense of spaciousness.

The moment you notice you were no longer aware, awareness has already returned —

stay with that recognition.

Perhaps at first you will notice thoughts, then sounds, then feelings — all of that is perfectly fine.

There is nothing to think — only to *be.*

Observe how this awareness, which perceives everything, never ceases — not when thoughts fade, not when feelings arise.

This is *You. This awareness is God within you.*

16

From Guilt to Grace – The Path of Self-Acceptance in the Heart of Jesus

The Illusion of Guilt – When One Forgets to Love Oneself
Human beings often approach God as if they were unworthy —
as though the Father's love were conditional, something to be
earned rather than something that has always been ours.

Yet Jesus revealed not the path of condemnation, but the path of forgiveness.

Guilt arises when we identify with our mistakes and forget that within us lives One who has never been tainted —

the Spirit, the conscious presence, the living Christ within.

The word *sin* comes from the Greek *hamartia* — "to miss the mark."

It does not mean that our essence is evil, but that our attention has turned in the wrong direction.

A person "sins" when they turn away from the Light —

but the Light never turns away from them.

Thus Jesus did not ask us to be afraid, but to return to the Source —

for we were never truly cast out.

Guilt arises when we condemn within ourselves something we have thought, felt, or done.

Then the heart divides: one part accuses, the other defends, and we no longer experience the mistake itself, but the rejection of ourselves.

Yet thoughts, feelings, and desires are part of our human nature —
the waves of life's own movement.

The error is not that they appear, but that we judge them.

Too often we look into the world's mirror and see a distorted image,

believing we are less than we are because someone once made us believe so.

But that mirror is not the truth.

In the depths of the soul, every human being is innocent — even when they stumble —

for mistakes are the path of growth.

Guilt dissolves when we understand: we are not bad, but on the way home, and the divine light comes to know itself through our experiences.

> "Judge not, and you shall not be judged;
>   condemn not, and you shall not be condemned;
>   forgive, and you shall be forgiven." (Luke 6:37)

> "I came not to call the righteous, but sinners." (Matthew 9:13)

In saying this, Jesus liberated humanity from the bondage of guilt.

Our faults are not fatal marks, but teachers.

Through the light of awareness we come to realize:

you are not your mistake — you are the one who sees it.

And that witnessing awareness is Christ within you.

Just as when Jesus stood before the woman caught in adultery, and when He spoke with the Samaritan woman at the well (John 4:1–26), both stories reveal the same love.

At the well, Jesus rests in the heat of the day. When the woman comes to draw water, He says to her, *"Give me a drink."*

The woman is astonished — for a Jewish man not only speaks to her, but even asks something from her.

Yet Jesus reveals the deeper meaning of thirst:

"If you knew the gift of God, and who it is that says to you, 'Give me a drink,' you would have asked Him, and He would have given you living water."

Gradually the woman understands that Jesus is not speaking of physical water, but of the Spirit — the living presence that can forever quench the inner thirst of the soul.

This encounter is a quiet example of forgiveness and acceptance.

Jesus does not condemn the woman for her past, though He knows she has had many husbands;

instead, He unveils to her the true source of longing.

Through love, He transforms shame into divine understanding.

Thus the woman who once hid from her town becomes the bearer of good news, calling others:

"Come, see a man who told me everything I ever did!"

At the well there is no judgment, but rebirth — through the outpouring of the living water, the Spirit.

Likewise, when Jesus faced those who wished to stone the adulterous woman, He did not respond with anger but with silence —

the silence of divine wisdom:

"Let the one among you who is without sin be the first to throw a stone at her." (John 8:7)

This story remains an eternal image of mercy and the absence of judgment.

In it, Jesus reveals that the heart of God does not lean toward punishment, but toward understanding and restoration.

Here guilt melts away in the light of love, for the Spirit recognizes that God always looks into the deepest part of the heart —

and there He finds nothing but the longing to return Home.

The Call to Forgiveness – God Never Gives Up on You

Every act of Jesus carried the message of forgiveness.

He did not merely *teach* about love — He *embodied* it.

The crucifixion was not the fulfillment of wrath, but the revelation of mercy.

Where the world judged, Jesus loved.

Where others would have turned away, He turned toward.

"Father, forgive them, for they do not know what they are doing." (Luke 23:34)

Within this single sentence lies the dissolution of every human error.

Ignorance is the root of all sin.

When a person forgets who they truly are — a child of God's light — they fall into error.

But God sees the innocence beneath our ignorance, and for that reason He never gives up on us.

There is always the possibility of awakening, of turning back, of returning to the original innocence from which we came.

The Prodigal Son and the Father's Heart – The Joy of Coming Home

The parable of the prodigal son is the deepest proof that God does not judge — He waits for us to come home.

The Father did not wait for the son to apologize or to prove he had changed.

When He saw him from afar, He was already running toward him.

This is the movement of divine love: forgiveness is swifter than repentance.

"While he was still a long way off, his father saw him, and was filled with compassion for him; he ran to his son, threw his arms around him, and kissed him." (Luke 15:20)

This moment contains an eternal truth: God does not reject — He receives.

Even before you utter a word of self-blame, the divine embrace is already around you.

Human beings were given the freedom to err, because only through that freedom can we learn what love truly means.

Freedom, then, is not the path of disobedience, but the sacred space in which love is understood.

The Divine Goodness and the Nature of Light – The Misunderstanding of Hell

There is no vengeance in God, for love cannot contradict itself.

Hell is not the place of God's wrath, but the state of a consciousness that turns away from the light.

Darkness is not something sent by God — it is simply the absence of light.

God is goodness itself, light itself, life itself — and these can only flow outward.

Light never condemns darkness; it silently illumines it.

When one realizes that the goodness of God embraces all things, the fear of judgment dissolves.

One understands that there is nothing to escape from.

Light does not pursue — it invites.

Love does not accuse — it lifts up.

In this realization, guilt within the heart is transformed into gratitude.

The Awakening of Consciousness – The Art of Divine Self-Acceptance

Conversion is not a moral achievement, but the awakening of consciousness.

When you realize that God lives not outside of you but *within* you, everything changes.

Guilt contracts the heart, but realization opens it.

Forgiveness is not an act of logic, but of breath — the breath of God that restores life to the soul.

"Whoever comes to me I will never cast out." (John 6:37)

Self-acceptance, therefore, is not self-justification, but seeing what God sees in you.

When Jesus looks at you, He does not see your past — He sees your origin.

Not the sinner, but the child.

And in that moment, you too become a child again in the eyes of the Father.

One who truly understands the teaching of Jesus realizes that guilt is not a sign of humility, but a misunderstanding of love.

True humility is not self-punishment, but the recognition that God already lives within you — and loves you exactly as you are.

You Are Not Sinful Because of What Is Within You, but Because of What You Do With It

In the teachings of Jesus, sin is not a moral label but a state of obscured consciousness.

Sin is not an invisible stain upon the soul, but the moment when awareness forgets itself — when the mind turns away from love.

For Jesus, sin was not so much an action as it was forgetfulness: the forgetting of who we truly are — the image of the Father, the consciousness of Love.

When a thought, emotion, or desire arises within us, it is not in itself sin.

It is the natural movement of consciousness.

The Spirit comes to know itself *through* human experience — through anger, desire, fear, and pain.

Jesus never condemned the feelings that arise within us, for He knew they are the very ground of growth.

Sin is born only when consciousness forgets itself and becomes fully identified with what it feels or thinks — when fear, rather than love, becomes the guiding force.

"Nothing that enters a person from the outside can defile them; rather, it is what comes out from within that defiles." (Mark 7:15)

This is one of Jesus's deepest psychological insights.

It is not external influence, nor thought, nor temptation that makes us impure, but the unconscious identification with what we feel.

When one believes, *"I am the anger, I am the desire, I am the judgment,"* awareness darkens, and actions begin to flow not from love, but from fear.

Sin, then, is not about *content* — it is about *identification*.

If you observe your thoughts and emotions without rejecting or identifying with them, they are brought into the Light.

The light of awareness purifies.

What becomes seen becomes free.

Sin exists only so long as it remains hidden from consciousness.

When you see it in the light of the Spirit, it can no longer harm you — for recognition itself is redemption.

But when you believe that you *are* the thought — when anger turns into "*I am*" — it condenses into shadow and takes form in action.

Sin, therefore, is nothing but the embodiment of love's absence within deeds.

According to Jesus, forgiveness is not a moral gesture, but the purification of consciousness from false identifications.

The one who truly forgives recognizes that there was never anything to forgive — for all was but the dream of ignorance.

Sin is only the soul's dream, in which love searches for itself.

Whoever realizes that sin has no true existence, being merely the absence of light, ceases to judge.

In the words of Jesus, "sin" is not simply a moral fault but *hamartia* — a missing of the mark, a loss of divine direction.

The one who sins is not evil, but lost; unable to see the true goal, which is love.

Every soul is moving toward love — only differing in the degree of remembrance.

The sinner and the righteous are not separated by morality, but by awareness: one has forgotten, the other remembers.

Yet both are carried by the same Light — the Light that speaks through Jesus' words:

"I did not come to judge the world, but to save it." (John 12:47)

Guilt, then, is not the voice of God, but the echo of the mind.

God does not accuse — He calls.

The place of guilt can be taken by recognition and love:

the recognition that even in our deepest errors, there lies hidden the longing to return to Oneness.

That recognition itself *is* purification.

Contemplation – Encounter with the Inner Christ

Close your eyes, and stand before Jesus.

Imagine Him looking at you — not seeing your faults, but the light within you that your past has never been able to dim.

Listen as He gently says:

"You are always with me, and all that I have is yours." (Luke 15:31)

Feel how His words softly dissolve the guilt you have carried for years.

See that your wounds are not marks of shame, but places where the light has entered.

Every mistake becomes an opportunity to experience love.

Grace is not a reward, but the very nature of the Divine — continual forgiveness and rebirth.

Then you realize: God is not a distant judge, but an inner Source who holds you in every fall.

You no longer need to fear Him, for He *is* Life itself — the One who desires *you*, not your perfection.

The awakening of grace is nothing less than the realization that God has never, not for a single moment, given up on you.

In every failure, in every misstep, He waits for you to see that His light has always burned within you — waiting only for you to open your heart and return home to Love.

17

The Mystery of Gratitude

Gratitude is not a mere emotion — it is a sacred realization.
When we feel gratitude, we awaken to Oneness itself — to the
truth that all that exists flows from God and continues to live within
us.

Most people feel grateful only when something pleasant happens to them.
But true gratitude is unconditional.

The heart that is truly awake is grateful even for what is difficult, because
it recognizes that every event serves the unfolding of the Spirit.

*"Everything that happens is in its rightful place. Everything that exists stands
within the order of God."*
— *Hermes Trismegistus, Corpus Hermeticum*

Gratitude lights a candle in the dark room of the mind.

When we turn our attention to what is already here, the illusion of lack
dissolves.

The heart opens and perceives that we have always lived in abundance —
we simply failed to notice.

Gratitude for What Is

Every breath we take is a gift.

Every day we live is an opportunity to love, to see, to create with awareness. You can be grateful for:

the air you breathe,

the light that illuminates your path,

the water that gives life,

the taste of food, where God's providence is hidden,

your body, which carries your soul,

the people who have accompanied, taught, loved, or tested you.

Every experience, every relationship has been a mirror of consciousness — to help you recognize that *you yourself are the Source.*

Gratitude for the Steps Along the Way

We often forget how much we have already survived.

But when we look back, we can see:

there was always an invisible hand sustaining us.

Every obstacle you have overcome, every pain you have endured, has shaped you — it was the hand of God working within you.

Here gratitude becomes transmutation: when you can see blessing even in the wounds of the past.

"The Soul loses nothing, for every experience increases its richness."

— *Hermetic Teaching*

Gratitude for Humanity

Be grateful for those who came before us.

Every house we live in, every book we read, every word we understand — all are gifts from generations past.

They laid the foundations of knowledge, faith, and love.

As Hermes wrote:

"Whoever is grateful to their ancestors honors the chain of the Divine Order, for every spirit proceeds from the One."

Humanity is a single great breath — countless bodies, but one Soul.

When you are grateful for others, you are grateful for yourself within the

Unity.

Gratitude to God – The Source

In the end, all gratitude returns to God.

For He is the One through whom we breathe, see, love, and create.

The prayer of gratitude is not a request, but a realization:

"All things come from You, and all things return to You."

In the words of Jesus:

"To those who give thanks, more will be given; but from those who do not recognize, even what they have will be taken away."

(paraphrased from Matthew 13:12)

Gratitude, then, is not only a spiritual practice — it is *theurgy*: the awakening of divine consciousness within us.

For when you are grateful, God flows through you into the world.

And then the miracle happens:

it is not the world that changes — *you* become the light.

Contemplation – Practice of Gratitude

Close your eyes.

Take three deep breaths.

Then think of three things present in your life right now for which you can be grateful.

They need not be great things — your heartbeat, the light through the window, a memory that brings a smile.

Every act of existence is a miracle.

And you are part of it.

"Whoever feels gratitude dwells in God."

III

Unity and Conscious Living

18

The State of Oneness – The Soul's Return to the Source

The Illusion of Separation

The deepest pain a human being carries is neither physical nor emotional — it is *ontological.*

It is the pain of believing ourselves to be separate from the One who created us.

This sense of separation is not sin, but a dream — a dream of division in which the human experiences itself as "outside" of the Whole.

Yet this dream lasts only until consciousness begins to turn back upon itself.

For the moment the gaze turns inward, something is seen that does not fade: *Presence.*

This Presence is not a "thing," but a *Someone* — and yet it is the most intimate essence of who we are.

The mystics have always proclaimed:

humanity does not find God *outside*, but exactly where it has never thought to look — in the depths of its own consciousness.

"Whoever knows himself knows God."

— *Hermes Trismegistus, Poimandres*

Interpretation:

This is one of the central truths of Hermetic wisdom.

The illusion of separation arises from the absence of self-knowledge — when one truly recognizes their own essence, they simultaneously recognize God, for the same Being is reflected within.

The Homecoming of the Soul

The purpose of the contemplative life is not the acquisition of knowledge, but *the return.*

It is not a movement forward, but a deepening inward.

The soul is not seeking something new, but something it has never truly lost — only forgotten: *Oneness.*

This Oneness is not a union between two separate beings, but the realization that there were never two to begin with.

Homecoming is a slow and gentle unfolding.

At first, it may come only in brief moments — in silent awareness, in a tear, in wordless presence.

Then it begins to appear more often, as the mind learns humility and the heart grows patient.

In the end, the soul no longer seeks distinctions, but *presence.*

It no longer holds questions, but *silence.*

And that silence is God Himself.

Oneness Is Not an Experience, but Reality

Many seek the *experience* of oneness.

Yet every experience arises and passes away.

Oneness is not like that.

It is not something we *experience,* but the reality in which we *exist.*

When we say we have had an "experience of unity," it is only that a window briefly opened to what has always been present.

The true realization of Oneness is not a moment of ecstasy, but of recognition.

Not a feeling, but a seeing.

When we no longer look *at* things, but recognize the One who *sees through us* —

then we understand: it has always been He who was seeing within us.

This state is not euphoria, but peace.

Not ecstasy, but simplicity.

And yet — it permeates everything.

The Nature of the State of Oneness

In this state, one no longer seeks God — for one recognizes there is no separation.

Prayer becomes silence.

Meditation becomes presence.

Seeking becomes fulfillment.

A person no longer lives *in* the world — the world lives *within* them.

Consciousness is no longer contained in the body; rather, the world floats within the vastness of awareness, like a sacred image.

Thoughts arise, yet they no longer disturb.

Feelings appear, yet they do not carry one away.

The body moves, yet without urgency.

Time itself begins to slow, until it finally dissolves — and only the eternal *Now* remains.

This *Now* is not a fleeting moment, but pure *Presence* —

the *"I Am"* in whom the world exists.

Meditation on Union with God

Anyone who reads the Gospels attentively will notice that silence and reflection suffused Jesus' life. Although Scripture does not use the word "meditation" in the modern sense, everything we today mean by that word is present in Jesus' practice: mindful presence, immersion in the divine

Presence, the quiet prayer before God—not as something outward, but as an inner reality.

The Gospels repeatedly say that Jesus "withdrew by himself" — to the mountain, to the wilderness, or to the shore of the sea. This withdrawal was not an escape but a return: into the Father's arms, into the inner silence where every prayer ceases to be words and the Soul prays to the Soul.

> *"And when he had sent the multitudes away, he went up into the mountain apart to pray: and when the evening was come, he was there alone."*
> *(Matthew 14:23)*

This sentence is a perfect image of the essence of meditation. The mountain here is not merely a geographic place but the height of consciousness: that inner point where one leaves the noisy world and enters the realm of silence. That Jesus "was there alone" means the roles and masks of the world fell away, and only Pure Presence remained: the "I Am" who is in the Father.

Elsewhere we read:

> *"And in the morning, rising up a great while before day, he went out, and departed into a solitary place, and there prayed."*
> *(Mark 1:35)*

This pre-dawn prayer also symbolizes the inner dawn of the soul: the turning from darkness toward light. Jesus prayed not only with words but with his whole being. When his disciples later saw him, they often felt an otherworldly peace emanating from him — the radiance of that deep presence in which he bathed day by day.

When he sat alone on the shore of the Sea of Galilee, he did not merely rest but contemplate: the waves mirrored the consciousness of God, the whispering wind felt like the breath of the Holy Spirit. Every natural image spoke to him of the Father's voice. That state of awareness — alert, loving attention — is the deepest meditation: when one no longer thinks about God but becomes conscious of God within oneself.

"But he withdrew himself into the wilderness, and prayed."
(Luke 5:16)

This "withdrawing" is the return to the inner chamber of the heart, which Jesus himself taught:

"But thou, when thou prayest, enter into thy closet, and when thou hast shut thy door, pray to thy Father which is in secret; and thy Father which seeth in secret shall reward thee openly."
(Matthew 6:6)

This *"inner room"* is not a physical chamber but the depth of the soul — the quiet awareness in which the world's thoughts fall still.

Jesus was not merely the master of silence but of deep attention. When others spoke to him, he did not merely hear them; he listened with his whole being. Before his words there was always the attention of silence: the open field of the heart where every person's pain and joy had room. He did not judge but listened. He did not rush to reply, but allowed the Spirit to speak through him. Such listening itself was meditation — the state of presence in which one does not attend to one's own thoughts but to God, who speaks through the other's words.

When he said, *"He that hath ears to hear, let him hear"* (Matthew 11:15), he did not mean bodily hearing but the hearing of the soul — that inner attentiveness capable of discerning the divine truth behind form. And when he taught, *"Blessed are the pure in heart: for they shall see God"* (Matthew 5:8), he spoke of the purification of consciousness: the state in which the noise of thoughts subsides and the soul reflects the divine light clearly.

He named this inner state the key to the kingdom when he said:

"Except ye be converted, and become as little children, ye shall not

enter into the kingdom of heaven."
(Matthew 18:3)

The child here is not one of age but of the purity of mind: the innocent attention that judges not, compares not, fears not. The child is simply present — this is the soul-presence in which God recognizes Himself in the human. Jesus expressed the same inward truth when he said:

"Whosoever shall receive one such little child in my name receiveth me."
(Matthew 18:5)

And elsewhere:

"Inasmuch as ye have done it unto one of the least of these my brethren, ye have done it unto me."
(Matthew 25:40)

And when he said,

"For I was an hungred, and ye gave me meat; I was thirsty, and ye gave me drink; I was a stranger, and ye took me in; naked, and ye clothed me; I was sick, and ye visited me; I was in prison, and ye came unto me."
(Matthew 25:35–36)

he spoke not merely of acts of love but of the fact that He Himself dwells in every living being — the divine Soul, the Christ-consciousness, the light of pure presence.

He who feeds the hungry does not only help; in the action he meets God. He who cares for the sick passes on the touch of Christ, for Jesus is present in every sufferer as the silent witness of the Soul. He who listens to the lonely listens to Divine Consciousness itself — the presence that lives in every heart, waiting to be recognized.

Therefore he said: "Inasmuch as ye have done it unto one of the least of these my brethren, ye have done it unto me." These words are not merely moral exhortation but the deepest mystical insight: the teaching of unity. For the theurgic eye this means that every person and every being is the sacred temple of the Soul. One who sees in this way no longer separates oneself from another, for one knows that in every moment and in every relation God meets Himself.

Hence he said:
"I in them, and thou in me." (John 17:23)

In a single sentence he reveals the heart of theurgy: the unity of Soul and consciousness. One who lives in this deep, pure attention not only believes in God but becomes conscious in God.

Thus Jesus' life was not merely teaching but continual meditation — wakeful, loving attention in the Father's presence. And whoever follows him on this path will discover that divine love does not live in words but in that quiet awareness which hears all, sees all, and embraces all.

He became the living example that meditation is not withdrawal but the deepest form of life. It is not escape from the world but the recognition that God is present in everything — in the mirror of the water, in the touch of the wind, and even in suffering.

Therefore the follower of Jesus must not only pray but quietly "return to the mountain" — that is, to one's own heart where the Father dwells.

"Abide in me, and I in you." (John 15:4)

This is the summary of Jesus' meditation: not in words, but in abiding in the Soul. That deep, inner attention in which one no longer seeks God, because one recognizes that God has always lived within.

The Pull of Grace

Oneness is not the fruit of human effort.

No one can reach it through will alone.

The summit of the inner path is not conquest, but surrender.

When a person gives everything — including themselves — only that which has eternally been remains: *God.*

This surrender is not passive; it is the deepest act of trust.

One who falls into this trust is carried by grace itself.

There is no longer a need to grasp, no need to prove.

Only to *be.*

This being is participation in the being of God — it *is* Oneness itself.

The Hermetic sages taught that the Light never disappears — only consciousness turns away from it.

Like the sun that remains shining even when we stand in its shadow, the Light continues to radiate, unchanged.

Light is the symbol of divine presence — the eternal Consciousness that permeates all things, from which we can never be truly separated.

When the soul releases its striving — when it no longer seeks to ascend, to awaken, to achieve, or to prove — it steps out of the shadow.

The Light does not return from outside; it begins to shine from within.

This moment is not a human achievement, but the act of Grace itself.

For it is not humanity that finds God, but God who finds Himself within us.

The light of awareness, once veiled by the boundaries of the self, now reflects itself again — God gazing upon Himself in the heart of humankind.

This return is not an action, but a recognition; not a movement, but an opening.

Where will ceases, Grace begins.

There begins true *Theurgy* — when the soul no longer acts in search of God, but God acts within the soul, revealing Himself through it.

And in that revelation, all becomes One again:

the Light returns to itself, and consciousness realizes it has never been apart from the Source.

False Oneness and True Realization

When a person touches the Infinite, the ego often makes one last attempt to wear the face of God.

It whispers: *"I am God," "I am the source of light," "I stand above all things."*

But this is the final illusion — separation disguised as pride.

The one who truly unites with God does not rise above others, but bends down to all beings.

They do not seek to rule, but to serve.

They do not see themselves as superior, but perceive that they were never separate to begin with.

True realization is not power — it is *transparency.*

The soul no longer tries to possess the light, for it has itself become translucent, allowing the Light to shine through.

"Enlightenment" is not a triumph, but a blessed surrender — the recognition that the one who *sees* is rooted within the *Seen.*

In pure Presence of the Spirit, there is no death, for there is no one left to die.

All change is but transformation within the eternal flow of the Whole.

God does not stand apart from this flow — He *is* the Flow itself, the pulse of Being within every form.

The consciousness in which you are reading these words is His reflection within creation.

In every human being this light lies dormant — not as a reward, but as origin.

It is not something to gain, but something to uncover.

"If you bring forth what is of God within you, it will be light in you.

If you hide or reject it, that light slowly fades within — and the soul grows dim.

Yet even this darkness is no punishment, only a dream in which God patiently waits until you recognize Him again within yourself."

Realization, then, is not power — it is *homecoming.*

And one who has come home no longer questions, no longer strives, no longer wishes to be light —

for they know: they have always been so.

19

Mystical Union

Enlightenment and Sanctification
The deepest longing of the human soul is not merely peace or happiness, but *Oneness.*

It does not wish only to *know* God, but to *be united* with Him.

In Christian mysticism, this is called *sanctification*; in the Eastern traditions, *enlightenment.*

Though the words differ, they point to the same reality — the realization that there are no longer two, but only One.

Enlightenment is not a fleeting moment of illumination, but the deep seeing that the divine presence is what we truly are.

This vision does not occur through the eyes, but through the silent awakening of the heart.

It is not an inner experience that becomes the focus of attention, but rather the *awareness itself* that holds all experience.

Sanctification is not moral perfection, but life permeated by the Spirit — a state in which every thought, movement, and silence belongs to God.

This unity is not a rejection of the world, but its fulfillment in the light of God.

When one reaches this state, there is no more seeking approval, no proving, no striving.

The soul rests — as one who has come home.

The searching self yields to the divine *"I Am"* within.

This is not passivity, but the deepest alertness — when the person expands within presence and becomes one with it.

"God does not enter into the human being from outside; He was always there."

(*Paraphrase of the Gospel of Thomas, Saying 3*)

Teresa of Ávila, Meister Elkhart, and the Teaching of Buddhism

In her mystical visions, Saint Teresa of Ávila describes the soul's journey through the *interior castles,* until it reaches the innermost dwelling where nothing remains but God.

This is not merely poetic imagery, but an exact description of the state in which consciousness becomes completely purified, retaining only one intention: God.

Teresa speaks of the *fire* that does not burn, but transforms.

The innermost dwelling cannot be entered by force — only by letting love open the door.

Meister Eckhart expresses the same truth:

"At the deepest level, the soul of man is one with God."

He did not await heavenly visions but taught that when we let go of the "self," what remains is God Himself within us.

This emptying is not loss, but fullness.

"The quiet soul receives God more readily than knowledge," he said.

Where the self dissolves, God begins to live.

The Buddhist tradition, though born of another culture, speaks of this same natural state — the original purity of consciousness, which neither comes nor goes and is already perfect.

Nothing needs to be attained, only recognized.

The Christian mystic understands the same: God does not come — He reveals Himself when the heart lays down its own ideas.

All three traditions teach that we are not separated from God or from ourselves; we have only forgotten.

The Soul's Homecoming into God

The aim of the contemplative path is not new knowledge or new experiences, but the final *homecoming.*

The soul — having journeyed far from separation to presence — now realizes that God is not distant, but the very foundation of being.

Homecoming is not a movement but an awakening — the recognition that we have always been there.

Everything we sought was already present in the innermost heart.

This state is not ecstasy or endless suspension, but profound peace — a silence in which everything simply *is.*

The world is no longer "other," but transparent: in everything, the light of God shines.

A tree, a human gaze, a walk in the sunlight — all become the language of God.

No more questions are needed, for Being itself is the answer.

No striving is required, for the goal is within itself.

The soul no longer seeks — it gives thanks.

Everything becomes simple, everything unfolds naturally, and one knows: *"I and the Father are one."*

In this realization, the soul surrenders completely.

It no longer desires to *do,* but to *live from* God.

This life is not idle, but creative — for one who is one with God does not withdraw, but radiates.

The soul returns home to God — and lives no longer apart.

"The one who knows becomes one with what is known.
Whoever has come to know the Truth is free.

For the Truth is not outside of us, but within;
it is through Him that all knowing comes."
— Gospel of Philip, Saying 67

This Realization Is Not of Thought, but of Being

Here, *knowing* does not mean that consciousness takes possession of something,

but that it recognizes it has always been one with it.

In true knowing there is no distance, no subject and object,

no seeker and sought — only Oneness remains,

where Consciousness beholds itself in all things.

When a person comes to this vision, they do not gain new knowledge,

but return to what they have always been — the Source of knowing, which is God.

Thus the Gnosis declares: *"The one who knows becomes one with what is known."*

In the moment of knowing, God recognizes Himself within the human being.

And in that recognition, the person is free —

for duality ceases, and the search comes to an end.

Consciousness and Truth are one:

the Light beholds itself.

The Hermetic Wisdom of Light and Consciousness

According to the Hermetic sages, enlightenment is nothing other than the return of human consciousness to its divine origin.

Hermes Trismegistus teaches:

"Whoever knows himself knows God, for the divine essence is the same from which the human soul has come."

This realization is the essence of *Gnosis* — not the accumulation of knowledge, but the awakening to the Light that dwells within.

In Hermetic understanding, the human being is of dual nature: a mortal body and an immortal consciousness, a spark of the Divine Mind (*Nous*).

Enlightenment is not the perfection of the mortal part, but the recognition that we have never been separate from the Eternal.

"The Light of God shines in all things, yet it becomes visible only in the mirror of the purified heart."

(Corpus Hermeticum, *XI.20 – paraphrase*)

True sight is not the work of the eyes, but of the heart.

For Light does not arrive from outside — it ignites within us when consciousness becomes still and the Divine Mind returns into itself.

This is the divine vision, when *"the Light beholds itself."*

"In humankind, consciousness is the seed of the Divine Mind; when one realizes this, one becomes one with the Whole."

(*Corpus Hermeticum*, XIII.3–4 – paraphrase)

When the soul recognizes that the Light is not to be *attained* but *recognized*, the search ceases.

The human being no longer looks for God outside, but awakens to the truth that they are the very expression of divine consciousness.

This is the Hermetic *rebirth* — when one no longer lives according to the earthly mind, but from the Light through which all life exists.

In the words of Hermes:

"Whoever returns to the Light becomes divine, for the divine consciousness is no longer separate from them."

(Corpus Hermeticum, *XIII.14 – paraphrase*)

In this state, duality dissolves: there is no longer God and man, seeker and sought — only the One.

This is the shared essence of *sanctification* and *enlightenment:* when the soul realizes that it is itself the Light it has always sought.

Thus Hermetic wisdom fulfills the words of Jesus:

"I and the Father are one."

For whoever truly knows themselves recognizes God within — and in that recognition, all separation disappears.

20

The Mystic Christians

The Deepest Currents of Christian Mysticism
The most profound streams of Christian mysticism — where the soul directly experiences God — have always spoken of the purification of consciousness, the ascent of the soul, and the inward recognition of the Divine Presence.

The masters who walked the inner path of contemplation, silence, and divine union all pointed toward the same realization: that God is not outside of us, but dwells in the innermost reality of the soul.

Mystical Christianity is, therefore, the path of consciousness toward God — the way of awakening, in which a person realizes that they themselves are the expression of God in the world.

The Desert Fathers – The Legacy of Silence

The roots of Christian mysticism reach back into the silence of the desert.

When faith in the cities became an external form, some sought the inner life — those who withdrew into the desert not to hear the voices of men, but the voice of God.

These Desert Fathers — St. Anthony, Macarius, Poemen, Arsenius, and their companions — were the first cartographers of the soul's journey.

They did not write books; they lived their teachings, showing through their lives what true prayer means: presence in silence.

In the desert, everything unnecessary fell away.

Thoughts, desires, and justifications all faded, for nothing remained to feed them.

In that stillness, it slowly became clear that the soul's true home is not in the world, but in God.

For them, the desert was not escape, but return — to the simplicity before Creation, where the human could again become what they had always been: the image of God.

Anthony's understanding of self-knowledge was not psychological analysis, but the realization of the soul's transparency.

One who no longer identifies with thoughts, emotions, or roles discovers within the source that has always been pure — the divine consciousness.

In the desert, this realization was not theory, but direct experience: when all becomes silent, the Spirit itself answers.

> "I have often regretted speaking, but never regretted keeping silent."
> — *Abba Arsenius*

Arsenius taught the theology of silence.

The one who learns to be silent is not fleeing the world, but awakening inner attention.

In silence, personal opinion and judgment fall away, and what remains is divine witness — the awareness present in all things.

The Desert Fathers taught not through words, but through silence, knowing that God does not speak in noise, but in the heart of stillness.

> "He who truly prays no longer knows that he prays."
> — *Abba Zosimos*

At this depth, prayer is no longer petition or thought, but *being itself.*

When the mind falls silent, prayer prays itself within us — the Spirit prays within the Spirit.

In this state, the distinction between the one who prays and the One to whom they pray dissolves — all becomes a single presence.

This is the true legacy of the Desert Fathers: not doctrine or dogma, but divine life shining in the silence of consciousness.

The desert, therefore, is not a place, but a state of being.

Whoever turns inward enters the desert: the emptiness where nothing remains to hold on to — only pure Being itself.

Yet in that emptiness, God becomes visible.

Words fall away, and only Silence remains — the Silence in which the Divine Presence can be recognized.

And the one who, in that silence, recognizes themselves is no longer a separate being,

but the echo of the Eternal Light within creation.

Saint Augustine – The Recognition of the Inner God

"Do not go outward; return within yourself, for truth dwells in the inner man." – *Saint Augustine*

Saint Augustine stands as one of the earliest and most luminous witnesses of the inner path to God.

Before the language of mysticism or consciousness was ever defined, he had already glimpsed its essence — that the human soul is not a creation apart from God, but His living reflection.

When a person turns inward, beyond the noise of thought and the shifting images of the mind, they discover at the heart of awareness an eternal stillness — *the Presence that is Truth itself.*

Augustine called this the *interior light,* the divine essence that "illumines every mind." It is not something the intellect can grasp, for it is what makes the intellect capable of seeing.

The Truth he speaks of is not a concept to be known, but a living reality to be recognized — the very consciousness in which knowing occurs.

To *return within yourself* is therefore not withdrawal from the world, but awakening to its divine ground.

This inner turning is a movement from dispersion to unity, from the multiplicity of appearances to the One who sustains them all.

It is the soul's homecoming to the Source from which all things flow — the quiet recognition that *God was never absent, only unnoticed.*

In Augustine's vision, sin and suffering arise from *aversio Dei* — the turning away from God toward the transient.

Whenever the mind clings to what passes, it forgets the eternal; it mistakes the shadow for the light.

But when the attention becomes sanctified — when it rests again in the divine Presence rather than in the restless world of forms — the soul is healed.

This is the very practice of *awareness*: the act of remembering God through the simple grace of being present.

To be aware, then, is to pray without words.

In the silence beneath thought, the soul listens — and in that listening, God speaks.

The movement of prayer becomes the movement of awareness itself: the gaze turning inward until it beholds the Light that has always shone there.

Augustine's mystical teaching prefigures the later wisdom of the contemplatives — Eckhart's "divine spark," Teresa's "interior castle," the Hermetic Light that "sees itself."

All point to the same revelation he uttered in the language of faith:

that God and Truth dwell within, and to find them we must not ascend or strive outward, but *descend into the heart*, where eternity touches time.

The recognition of the Inner God is thus not an act of intellect, but of awakening.

It is the moment when the seeker realizes that what they sought has always been seeking through them.

And in that realization, the words of Augustine become a living experience:
"You were within me, but I was outside; and there I sought You...
You called and cried out, and broke open my deafness;
You flashed and shone, and dispelled my blindness."
— *Confessions, Book X*

In this awakening, the soul no longer reaches for God, for it has remembered:

the Light it sought *was itself the seeing.*

Master Eckhart – The Divine Spark

"God wishes to be born in every soul."
– **Master Eckhart**

Master Eckhart, one of the deepest thinkers of Christian mysticism, spoke of the *"divine spark"* (*funkelein*) that lies within the depths of every human soul.

This spark is always pure, unchanging, and untouched — the eternal light of consciousness through which God continually reveals Himself.

According to Eckhart, the true life of the soul begins when this divine birth takes place — when a person realizes that they are not a separate being, but that God's own life is expressing itself through them.

Pure awareness is the experience of this very "birth": the moment we recognize that the consciousness through which we see, hear, and perceive *is* the divine Life itself.

Eckhart's words remain timeless: God does not come to us from the outside, but is born within when the mind grows silent and the heart opens.

Saint Teresa of Ávila – The Interior Castle

"The soul is an interior castle in which God dwells in the innermost chamber." – *Saint Teresa of Ávila*

Saint Teresa of Ávila's mystical visions and writings describe the soul's gradual purification and ascent toward divine union.

Her image of the *"interior castle"* is a living symbol of this journey — a map of the soul's return from outward attachments and false identities toward the radiant stillness at its center, where God Himself abides.

Each chamber of this castle represents a deeper level of awareness.

At first, the soul still wanders among the outer rooms — absorbed in thoughts, emotions, and the echoes of the world.

But as the seeker turns inward, layer by layer, illusion by illusion, the noise of the outer life begins to fade.

What remains is the subtle light of presence — a growing intimacy with the divine essence that was never truly absent.

Reaching the *"seventh mansion"* marks the full union of the soul with God — the point where the "I" and the "Thou" dissolve into one luminous Being.

Here, prayer becomes effortless, for it is no longer the soul that prays, but God who breathes and loves within it.

The divine life flows freely, as the soul becomes transparent to the Light that fills all creation.

This inner pilgrimage parallels the modern understanding of consciousness.

The practitioner leaves behind layer after layer of identification — thoughts, roles, memories, the illusions of past and future — until arriving at the stillness of pure presence.

In this silence, God no longer appears as *someone* to be reached, but as *the very light of being itself*, shining through every form.

Teresa's *Interior Castle* is not merely a spiritual metaphor, but a revelation of the architecture of the soul.

It shows that sanctification and enlightenment are not separate paths, but two languages describing the same reality:

the awakening of consciousness to its divine center.

To enter the castle is to return home.

And the deeper one goes, the simpler everything becomes — until the soul realizes that the center it sought was never distant, for the Beloved was always waiting in the heart's most silent room.

Saint John of the Cross – The Dark Night of the Soul

"The dark night is not punishment, but purification — so that the light of God may become receivable within us." – *Saint John of the Cross*

Saint John of the Cross revealed one of the most mysterious and essential stages of the mystical path — *the dark night of the soul.*

It is the passage through interior emptiness, when the soul loses all former supports and every certainty begins to fade.

The outer joys, the emotional consolations, even the sweetness of spiritual experience, all dissolve — leaving nothing but the raw presence of being itself.

Yet this darkness is not the absence of God; it is His hidden work within the soul.

The night purifies perception, stripping away the images and desires that once veiled the Infinite.

It is the silence before dawn — the sacred preparation by which the human heart becomes capable of receiving divine light.

On the path of awareness, this same process appears as the dissolution of the ego — the falling away of every personal identification.

As all forms fade, the only light that remains is God's own radiance — the pure consciousness of being.

In that emptiness, what once seemed loss is revealed as transformation: the dying of illusion so that truth may live.

John reminds us that suffering and uncertainty are not signs of grace withdrawn,

but its most intimate doorway.

The dark night is the shadow cast by approaching light —

the moment when the divine sun has already risen, but the soul's eyes are not yet accustomed to its brilliance.

The silence that is born in this night becomes the map of divine presence. For when all things fall away, what remains is not despair, but stillness — and in that stillness, the soul discovers that even the darkness is filled with God.

Johannes Tauler and Heinrich Suso – The Theology of Silence

"The greatest word is the one spoken by silence." – *Johannes Tauler*

"Whoever would reach God must fall silent — from the noise of the world, and even from their own thoughts." – *Heinrich Suso*

For these Rhineland mystics, silence was not the absence of speech or thought, but the sacred space in which the divine becomes perceptible.

The *inner silence* they described is the purification of consciousness from all forms, all names, and all judgments.

When a person quiets the noise of the world and opens their attention completely, they touch the depth that both Tauler and Suso called *God*.

This silence is the truest theology — not to know the divine through words, but through presence.

It is a knowledge born not of reasoning, but of *being*.

In this wordless communion, the soul does not reach out toward God — it simply becomes transparent enough for Him to shine through.

In modern language, this inner stillness mirrors the contemplative or meditative state — the moment when consciousness rests in itself, observing its own nature.

Thoughts arise and pass, sensations appear and fade, yet the awareness that sees them remains unmoving and vast.

This unchanging awareness *is* the divine presence itself —
the eternal Silence that speaks without sound, and through which all creation breathes.

Angelus Silesius – The Paradox of Divine Presence

"The rose blooms without why: it blooms because it blooms."
— *Angelus Silesius*

In these luminous words, Angelus Silesius expresses one of the deepest truths of Christian mysticism:
life exists not *for* a purpose, but *from* the fullness of being itself.
God does not move toward an end; He is the eternal unfolding of His own nature —
a ceaseless flowering of presence in every moment.
This "purposeless existence" is also the essence of pure awareness:
the boundless, peaceful space in which all things appear, blossom, and fade without any need for justification or cause.
Here, existence is its own joy, its own answer.
When all desire and striving come to rest, the consciousness that remains is simplicity itself —
the quiet radiance of being, untouched and complete.
This is the divine stillness that Silesius called the "birthplace of God in the soul,"
where nothing needs to be achieved because all is already whole.
Thus, God is not to be sought in time or form,
but in the timeless Now —
the ever-present flowering of existence that is always here,
always new,
and forever beyond why.

The Modern Interpretation – Consciousness as the Reflection of God

The experience of the Christian mystics and the modern understanding of consciousness point to the same timeless truth:

at the depth of existence lies an eternal, formless awareness in which all things appear.

This awareness does not *belong* to us — we *belong to it.*

Pure consciousness is the sacred space where God contemplates Himself within the human soul.

For the one who awakens to this realization, all duality dissolves:

the Creator and the created, the seer and the seen, are united in Presence.

"For in Him we live and move and have our being." — **Acts 17:28**

This single verse summarizes the essence of Christian mysticism:

we do not exist *apart* from God — all things live, move, and are through His being.

The practice of awareness — remaining present, awake, and accepting — is therefore not a human effort to *reach* God,

but the return to what has always been: God's own self-recognition within us.

This path does not belong to any religion, but to the deepest truth of the human soul:

the realization that *consciousness itself is the temple,*

and that the *present moment* is the eternal sanctuary.

The Early and Medieval Christian Mystics

Even in the earliest centuries of Christianity, saints and contemplatives recognized the importance of inner divine awareness.

The Egyptian desert hermits — the *Desert Fathers* such as **Saint Anthony** and **Saint Macarius** — were among the first true practitioners of conscious presence.

They taught that purity of soul and silence are the gates through which the voice of God becomes audible.

"He who knows himself, knows God." — **Saint Anthony**

These words express the deepest meaning of Christian self-knowledge:

within every person lives the divine image, waiting to be seen.

Self-knowledge is not psychological analysis, but the transparency of mind,

where the light of consciousness can reflect the presence of God.

The **Cappadocian Fathers**, especially **Saint Gregory of Nyssa**, carried this mystical lineage forward.

Gregory taught that the soul's journey is an endless approach to God —

for the Divine is infinite and can never be fully grasped.

"The one who moves toward God will never cease advancing, for divine goodness is boundless." — **Gregory of Nyssa**

This endless movement reveals the dynamic aspect of awareness:

consciousness never fixes itself, but continuously unfolds toward the Infinite.

For the Christian mystics, enlightenment was not a final destination,

but an eternal expansion within God — an ever-deepening participation in the divine life.

Among the early theologians, **Clement of Alexandria** and **Origen** emphasized that union with Christ begins with the purification of inner sight.

The cleansing of the mind is not an intellectual process, but a simplification of consciousness —

a focusing of love and attention into oneness.

"The pure heart is the one that sees the light of God in all things." — **Origen**

This teaching echoes directly the words of Jesus in the Sermon on the Mount:

"Blessed are the pure in heart, for they shall see God."

For the mystics of every age, this purity is not moral perfection,

but clarity of perception — the state in which awareness itself becomes divine vision.

In this way, from the early desert hermits to the contemplative theologians and the modern practitioners of mindfulness,

one thread unites them all:

the realization that the divine is not an external being to be sought,

but the luminous essence of consciousness itself —

the living mirror in which God eternally beholds His own face.

The East-Asian Medieval Christian Mystical Traditions

During the Middle Ages, Christianity journeyed along the Silk Road into China, India, and Central Asia.

There, the **Nestorian missionaries** — known in Chinese as the **Jingjiao**, the *"Religion of Light"* — sought to express the Christian revelation through the contemplative languages of Eastern philosophy.

These communities, largely of Syriac origin, united Christian mysticism with the inward depth of Taoist and Buddhist thought, translating the language of faith into the vocabulary of awakening.

"The radiance in which all forms appear is the Word of God — the eternal Light that illumines all things."
— **Jingjiao Stele, Xi'an, 8th century**

This ancient inscription from the celebrated Xi'an Stele, one of the earliest Christian monuments in China, reveals the heart of that mystical synthesis.

The very name *"Religion of Light"* points to the contemplative dimension of faith — the realization that divine presence does not shine from without, but radiates from within, illuminating the world from the inside out.

For the Nestorian Christians of the East, **Christ was the Light of the Cosmos**, dwelling in the consciousness of all beings as the inner brilliance of Life and Truth.

Prayer and contemplation were regarded as the tending of this *inner light*, the quiet cultivation of divine awareness in the soul.

Their writings often spoke of God as both *beyond* and *within* form — as the light that reveals all shapes yet is not bound by any of them.

In this way, they built a bridge between Christian theology and Eastern mysticism, affirming that **pure awareness** — the luminous clarity of mind — points everywhere to the same divine Source.

As the Gospel proclaims:

"Blessed are the pure in heart, for they shall see God." — **Matthew 5:8**

To these early contemplatives, purity of heart was not moral perfection, but the transparency of consciousness itself — the direct vision of God shining through all creation.

Thus the **prayer of the heart**, **silent contemplation**, and **unbroken presence** became, for them, the highest path:

the way by which the soul dissolves into union with the **divine Light** that lives within all things.

21

The Fabric of the Cosmos – The Law of Interconnection

The world is not a collection of separate parts, but a single living, breathing whole.

The air we breathe was born from the oceans' evaporation; the carbon and calcium in our bodies once burned in the hearts of stars.

Everything is connected to everything else, even if the human mind seldom perceives it.

Interconnection is not a poetic metaphor but a condition of being: every action ripples through the whole, for good or for harm.

Ancient wisdom called this *"the net of the cosmos"*: when you touch one strand, the entire web trembles.

Scientific and Philosophical Foundation

In the language of ecology, living beings and their environments form feedback systems; not a single thread can be pulled without the rest responding.

Our own bodies are such systems — heartbeat, breath, neural rhythms — each harmonizing to sustain life.

Systems theory, network science, and cybernetics reveal that the stability of the whole depends on patterns of relationship: homeostasis, balance, thresholds, and tipping points.

Reality, seen this way, is not made of isolated things but of relationships — and our attention tunes itself to those invisible threads.

The Buddhist View – Dependent Origination and Compassion

According to the Buddhist teaching of *dependent origination*, every phenomenon arises in relation to others.

Nothing exists independently; all things emerge within a web of causes and conditions.

This means that even the "self" is not an isolated entity but a network of relationships — of parents, teachers, air, water, sunlight, and countless other beings.

When this is deeply understood, compassion naturally awakens: if all is interconnected, no one's suffering is without consequence, and every act of love ripples outward through the world.

This insight is not theory but experience — when thought subsides, one can *feel* that life breathes as one.

Linked to dependent origination is the realization of *emptiness*: things have no fixed essence, and therefore remain open to change and healing.

Compassion — the wish that suffering be lessened — is not sentimentality but the clear seeing of our shared nature.

From this seeing arises the intent to extend goodness to all beings.

The Stoic Vision – Cosmic Unity (Sympatheia) and the Cosmopolis

The Stoic sages — Marcus Aurelius, Epictetus, and others — saw the cosmos as a single living organism ordered by the *Logos*, the divine Reason.

They called this deep coherence *sympatheia*: all things resonate together.

Every human being is a citizen of the *cosmopolis* — the universal city of the cosmos — where the measure of one's action is the common good.

When we live with this awareness, our actions cease to be self-centered; we understand that what serves the whole serves us as well.

Thus, Stoic compassion is not mere emotion but rational unity — the natural fruit of living in harmony with the greater order.

"All that happens is woven together; you yourself are a thread in the fabric of

the whole.

What benefits the community benefits you also." — **Marcus Aurelius, Meditations IV.40**

Another Stoic key is *oikeiōsis*: the widening of circles of care, from self to family, to city, to all humanity.

The wise person aligns their life with the Whole, understanding that these circles interpenetrate rather than exclude.

The Christian Mystical Vision – Divine Unity

In the teachings of Jesus, interconnection reveals itself as love:

"Whatever you did for one of the least of these brothers and sisters of mine, you did for Me."

This is not merely an ethical command but an ontological truth — the divine presence is the same in every being.

The Apostle Paul offers the same image: *"Many members, yet one body."*

If one member suffers, all suffer with it; if one is honored, all rejoice.

Even the mystery of the Trinity expresses this mutual indwelling — the eternal circulation of love (*perichorēsis*) — into which we enter whenever we love.

Love, then, is not a moral duty but a revelation: life is One, and we are all expressions of that One Life.

Ethical Implications – Responsibility Within Relationship

To perceive interconnection subtly yet deeply transforms daily ethics:

- **Speech:** Words do not vanish; they echo within relationships and within ourselves. Public speech shapes lasting structures of thought and emotion.
- **Consumption:** Every choice touches lives — people, animals, landscapes. Buying is a moral act.
- **Attention Economy:** What we attend to, we strengthen. The direction of our attention shapes the world; digital use is thus an ethical decision.

- **Ecology:** Overloading nature rebounds upon us; moderation is love for future generations.
- **Conflict:** Instead of demonizing others, we can perceive systemic causes — thus reconciliation and justice can coexist.

Everyday Practices – Experiencing Interconnection

- **Three Breaths with the World:** On the in-breath, recognize that the air comes from trees and oceans; on the out-breath, offer it back to all beings. Repeat three times.
- **Gratitude for Food:** Before eating, recall how many hands, soils, rains, and rays of light contributed to this meal. Taste one bite in full awareness.
- **Circle of Connection:** In thought, expand your heart outward — to family, friends, strangers, even those who challenge you — whisper inwardly: *"May you be well, may you be at peace."*
- **Ecological Choice:** Today, let one small decision (travel, packaging, meal) serve the whole. Notice how it feels to act with awareness of connection.
- **Listening Presence:** In conversation, practice complete attention. Do not advise; hold space. Attention heals, because it sustains the web.
- **Candle Meditation:**
- Imagine a warm flame glowing in your heart — the flame of awareness and love.
- With each breath it grows steadier and brighter.
- Now imagine lighting another person's candle with yours — your light does not diminish, but both flames shine stronger together, illuminating the space around you.
- One by one, you kindle more lights — loved ones, strangers, even those with whom you struggle.
- The light expands until it fills the whole world.
- Feel that the same flame burns in every heart — the fire of love and compassion that cannot be extinguished but multiplies in the darkness.
- **Journal of the Common Good:** Each evening, note how you contributed

(even in small ways) to the well-being of the whole, and how others supported you in return.

Common Misunderstandings and Clarifications

- *"If everything is connected, then nothing matters."*
- Not so — interconnection increases responsibility, for every act reverberates through the web.
- *"Compassion is weakness."*
- On the contrary, it is strength — a clearer perception of reality that enables right action.
- *"The common good opposes individual good."*
- In the short term they may appear to conflict, but in the long term they sustain one another — this is the logic of the cosmopolis.

The Power of Realization

When this truth is truly felt, the world is no longer an enemy but a kinship. Nature is not an object, but a relative.

Every encounter becomes sacred, for in every relationship the divine reflects itself.

Anger and fear begin to dissolve: we see that what we wound in another, we wound in ourselves; what we heal in another, we heal within.

Contemplative Question

"If everything you give ultimately returns to you, how would you live today?"

IV

Love and Compassion

22

Love and Compassion as the Ground of Consciousness

Compassion is not merely an emotional quality — it is the natural expression of consciousness itself.

When we observe life attentively, even in its smallest gestures, we can see that every living being instinctively avoids suffering and seeks happiness.

When we blink to keep our eyes from drying, when we shift our body to find comfort, when we long to eat, drink, or rest — all of these are expressions of the same impulse: the wish not to suffer, and the innate movement toward well-being.

This fundamental impulse is nothing other than a natural form of love and compassion toward ourselves.

When we truly see this within, we begin to understand: the same process unfolds in everyone else.

Every being seeks happiness and strives to avoid pain — though our means and paths may differ.

This realization awakens a deep compassion, for we begin to see that those who err, who grow angry, or who cause harm are in truth trying to lessen their own suffering — they simply do not know how.

From this insight arise understanding and forgiveness.

Beneath every thought, every action, every desire flows the same source: **love and compassion.**

We often fail to recognize it, because the mind distorts it — turning it into fear, possession, or defense.

But when we look deeply into our intentions, we find these two forces behind everything we do.

Love is what connects; compassion is what heals.

Together they form the divine nature of consciousness — the inner light that shines in every human being, whether it is recognized or not.

Love is not merely an emotion, but the deepest movement of existence itself — the impulse to give life and to connect.

Everything we do arises, in the end, from this — even error, anger, and fear are but obscured forms of love.

The soul comes from love, and to love it returns.

When we realize that within every person lives this same longing — the desire to connect, to be happy, to be free from pain — the world ceases to appear as a collection of strangers or enemies.

It becomes one living heart — a single breath of compassion pulsing through all.

The Expansion of Love

When we become aware of this fundamental energy within us, love naturally begins to expand — not only toward those we cherish, but even toward those with whom we experience difficulty.

Through mindful attention, love does not diminish; it grows.

For love is not possession, but flow.

The more we allow it to move through us, the more we realize that love is not something we *do* — it is what we *are.*

If you think you dislike yourself, or that you lack love, pause and ask: *Why did you buy this book? Why do you wish to change?*

That very wish already reveals love — the desire for goodness, for ease, for the feeling of being held and whole.

Even when you are dissatisfied with yourself or with life, the background of every thought and feeling is love itself —

for love is the root impulse that gives birth to all experience.

Sometimes the mind's filters darken this light — shaping it into fear, judgment, or restlessness —

yet the essential quality beneath remains self-love and compassion.

To recognize this is to dissolve the illusion of separation.

When we see that the same force moves in every heart, the "other" is no longer a threat, but a mirror.

The one who suffers longs for relief from the same source as we do.

The one who harms is trying, however blindly, to ease their own pain.

And the one who loves — reflects the face of God.

Conscious Compassion

Compassion is not pity — it is the recognition of our shared human nature.

When we see that others live from the same love and the same fears as we do, superiority and judgment dissolve.

We understand that every human being seeks happiness and well-being, and tries to avoid suffering — even when they stray onto mistaken paths.

Error is not a sign of malice, but of ignorance — of one who cannot yet see the consequences of their actions, or who does not know the true way to peace.

Often a person acts with good intentions, yet their thoughts and feelings distort reality through a clouded mirror.

From their own pain, they may even cause harm — not out of evil, but out of blindness.

As Jesus said upon the cross:

> *"Father, forgive them, for they know not what they do."*
> — **Luke 23:34**

These words speak not only of forgiveness, but of the highest manifestation of **conscious compassion**.

Here, Jesus reveals that true love is not bound to actions but to the soul itself:

it sees beyond ignorance to the goodness hidden within, the divine spark that lives in every human being.

This is the heart of deep compassion —

when we no longer see error, but misunderstanding;

no longer see an enemy, but a brother or sister who has lost their way.

Such compassion is not weakness, but the power of divine love that perceives through illusion and recognizes light even in darkness.

When we live in this vision, we ourselves become that very light —

the light of forgiveness, understanding, and unconditional love that spoke through the words of Jesus.

Compassion is not fragility; it is the deepest strength, for it dissolves the walls the ego builds.

To practice love and compassion is not a separate spiritual task — it is the natural functioning of awakened consciousness.

When we rest in silence and simply *observe*, the heart opens by itself, like a flower in sunlight.

We need not force it; we need only allow what has always been there to blossom once more.

A Deeper Understanding of Harmful Actions – The Roots of Misperception and Suffering

When a person forgets that they were born from love, fear becomes their compass.

Fear is not the absence of love, but its distorted reflection — for it, too, arises from the same source.

It is love's instinctive attempt to protect: to guard the body, the loved ones, and life itself.

Fear is the expression of love before it sees clearly — before it can distinguish what truly threatens from what exists only in the mind.

One who fears is not seeking evil, but safety.

One who defends or attacks is trying to protect something — their peace, their dignity, their relationships, or simply their life.

Thus, fear is not the enemy, but *love misunderstood* — the part of love that does not yet know there is nothing to fear, for at the depth of life, everything is held and safe.

When consciousness loses its connection to the divine trust within, fear takes control, and the movement of love becomes narrow and reactive.

From fear arise possession, anger, avoidance, and harm — all the forces that divide.

But when we look deeper, we see that behind every distorted act hides the same wish: that someone might be well, though they do not know how to bring it about.

The one who harms does not seek evil, but tries to ease their pain.

The one who errs is not corrupt, but blind — and blindness is the deepest form of suffering.

Thus, compassion is not excuse, but *seeing*: the recognition that behind every twisted act lies the longing for love.

Just as darkness has no existence of its own, but is only the absence of light, so too every sin, fear, and anger arises from the misperception of love.

This is why Jesus looked upon them not with judgment, but with love —

because He knew that sin is not the opposite of light, but the forgetting of it, and that every soul ultimately longs to return to the light.

When you realize that you are the vast, clear presence of awareness —

not merely the body or the mind, but the consciousness that pervades all things — fear begins to dissolve.

Not because you force it away, but because it comes into the light.

Fear cannot survive the quiet illumination of awareness: when you allow it to be, without resistance or suppression, it melts into the spaciousness that you truly are.

Conscious presence is therefore not a struggle against fear, but an awakening to the truth that you have always been safe.

One who sees in this way no longer hates, for they recognize that even behind fear, love is at work.

They no longer defend, for they feel that at the heart of life, all beings are protected.

And they no longer judge, for they know that the one who has gone astray is not an enemy, but a brother or sister —

journeying, by another road, toward the very same love.

The Reflection of Divine Love in Every Being

Love and compassion dwell within us because God Himself lives within us.

They are not inventions of the human mind, nor qualities we create — they are the movement of the Spirit, the pulse of divine life permeating all creation.

The blinking of the eye, the motion of the body, the rhythm of the breath — all are signs of divine providence at work within us.

Love is not merely a human trait, but the foundational vibration of existence itself — a universal resonance expressed through every living being.

When we adjust our posture to find comfort, it is the protective power of divine life moving within us.

When we thirst or long for rest, it is the self-love of God acting through us — the desire of existence to return to harmony with itself.

This love and compassion are not moral virtues, but divine light — an eternal flame burning in every heart.

Whoever recognizes this begins to see that in every human being, God's love moves the desires, the choices, and even the mistakes.

For every striving — even the most misguided — is ultimately the soul's attempt to return to the Source from which it came.

Behind anger lies the longing for peace; behind possessiveness, the yearning for safety; behind fear, love's obscured reflection.

When we see this, judgment falls away.

We understand that behind every human action, the same divine spark is at work — the same light that lives within ourselves.

Just as sunlight appears differently through each window yet remains the same light, so does God's love appear uniquely in every person, yet it is always one and the same.

Thus, compassion is nothing less than *seeing through the eyes of God.*

And love is not an emotion, but God's own presence within us — the ceaseless flow of divine life expressing itself through the world.

When we allow this love to move through us freely, we no longer merely *love* — it is God loving through us, God meeting Himself within His creation.

Then the words of Jesus are fulfilled:

"*Whoever abides in Me, and I in them, bears much fruit.*" — **John 15:5**

For the fruits of love and compassion do not come *from* us,
but are the continual unfoldings of divine life *within* us.

The Expansion of Love

Just as one candle can light another, so too does love spread.

When we turn toward others with awareness, the resonance of our hearts begins to touch them.

A gentle glance, a patient listening, a compassionate gesture — these are all ways in which love extends itself through the world.

When we live in this way, others can sense the peace within us, and it awakens in them the same spark of love.

This love is not a personal possession, but the flow of divine consciousness through creation.

When we open ourselves to it, it can move through us as well.

And as this awareness awakens in more and more people, the world itself begins to transform.

Practices for Recognizing and Expanding Love and Compassion

(15–20 minutes per day for 1–2 weeks)

1. Recognizing It Within Yourself

Sit quietly for a few minutes and observe how your body and mind respond to discomfort.

Notice that every small movement — a blink, a sigh, a shift in posture —

is an attempt to reduce suffering.

Recognize this as your basic self-love, the natural working of compassion within you.

2. Recognizing the Universal Desire

Bring to mind others — your family, your friends, strangers you have seen on the street.

See that they too long for happiness and seek to avoid pain.

This realization gives birth to compassion in the heart — a compassion that does not judge, but understands.

3. Expanding Love

Imagine a warm, golden light radiating from your heart, filling your body and then gradually extending outward.

First to those you love, then to those who are neutral to you, and finally to those with whom you struggle.

Silently repeat within:

"May you be happy. May you be free from suffering. May there be peace in your heart."

This love is not imagination — it is the true nature of consciousness, radiating in all directions.

4. Sustaining Compassion in Daily Life

Throughout the day, notice moments of care, attentiveness, and patience in yourself and in others.

See how people work to support their families, how hobbies and small joys restore their energy.

These are all expressions of compassion.

When you notice them, silently give thanks and allow them to grow stronger within you.

The light of attention brings growth wherever it is directed.

Bonus Practice – Loving-Kindness Meditation

Sit quietly, upright yet relaxed.

Bring your attention to the space of the heart, and if it helps, visualize it glowing with a warm golden light.

Breathe calmly.

Begin with yourself — take a few moments to recognize your own goodness and your capacity for peace.

Then, gently repeat:

"May there be peace within me."

"May I be safe."

"May I be happy and free."

Let each phrase sink deeply into your heart before repeating it again.

Next, bring to mind someone you love and repeat:

"May there be peace within you."

"May you be safe."

"May you be happy and free."

Then turn your attention to a neutral person, and finally to someone with whom you feel tension or difficulty —

offering each of them the same sincere wishes for peace, safety, and freedom.

If you have time, expand this circle outward —

to your neighborhood, your city, your country, and finally to the entire world.

Do not worry if you feel little at first; the practice itself cultivates the inner resonance that aligns your heart with the heart of God.

As a flower naturally turns toward the sun, so does the human heart open to the light of love.

The Meditation of Love and Recognition

Awakening Inner Forces

When I began these practices, I gradually started to recognize these forces within myself, and later in others as well. In each moment, I discovered new insights about myself, and as I delved deeper into these experiences, I noticed that the same forces were present in those around me, constantly at work, shaping and refining us. This experience was transformative: I developed a deeper understanding of myself, and simultaneously, I began to see others with greater clarity and sensitivity.

The Growth of Compassion

My compassion grew continuously, almost imperceptibly, without any sense of force; it unfolded naturally within me, like a gently growing light illuminating my inner landscape and subtly highlighting every nuance of my being. I realized that the effects of these practices extended beyond my inner self to the environment around me: my relationships became infused with empathy, patience, understanding, and acceptance. This subtle flow was perceived by others as well, reflecting back and strengthening mutual harmony and cooperation.

Connecting With Others

I observed how this force was at work in others, allowing me to approach them in everyday life with ease, love, and compassion—in the smallest gestures, the softest words, the quietest smiles—creating new harmony and deeper connection. I always begin with recognition, and it immediately illuminates why they act as they do, because they too wish to be happy, feel good, and avoid suffering. They seek safety, free from discomfort, uncertainty, and problems. I sense each person's motivation and inner state as they are in that moment, which brings complete understanding, clarity, and inner peace, as if the vibrations of every being in the world align with my own.

When Meditating

When I perform this meditation, I first recognize this state within myself and then expand it, feeling as if I am floating with others in a loving space, immersed in the flow of love and kindness. This recognition fills me with profound emotion. I do not always experience cathartic love or intense compassion; what matters most is the recognition itself. The feeling emerges at a more elemental level, allowing me to act and genuinely wish goodness for others. No feeling is ever forced, as that would only create a sense of obligation.

Seeing the Divine in Others

In these moments, I see the hearts of people, as Jesus taught, and recognize in them pure consciousness, their presence of soul, the Divine light residing in all of us—always invisible yet present, gently guiding us on the path of love and understanding. Even when I encounter poor or suffering people on the street, I perceive the same in them: the untouched consciousness and divine love radiating through their everyday life and presence. It reminds me that every soul is valuable, every moment sacred, and every encounter an opportunity to learn and extend love.

Continuous Practice

I continue to practice these exercises to this day, knowing that recognition must remain alive to grow ever stronger, deeper, and broader. Each day, it refreshes the harmony of my mind and heart, while the flow of love and compassion continues to expand and enrich my being and those around me.

23

The Outpouring of Love – The Path of Divine Action

Divine Oneness Does Not Withdraw

The one who has truly entered the contemplative union no longer seeks to retreat from the world — they overflow. Divine presence is not a static state but a living current. Like a spring that does not hold its water but lets it become a river, so the Spirit within us flows: born of love, moving outward as love into the world.

This divine outpouring does not arise from intention or moral effort, but from nature itself. When presence deepens, it begins to act. It is not *we* who do, but the Presence — who we truly are — that begins to move. This is contemplative action: silent, gentle, unnoticeable — yet transforming the whole world.

Love as Movement, Not Emotion

In the world, many feelings are called love, but divine love is not a mood or an emotion. It does not depend on what we feel but on what we open to. Divine love is the soul's natural movement beyond itself. Love does not strive — it flows. It does not accumulate — it gives. It does not possess — it *is*.

When this is recognized, love ceases to be an effort and becomes an effortless flow. It needs no force, only permission. Like a tree that bears fruit not by will but by harmony with soil, sun, and water — so love ripens in us when our consciousness is rooted in God.

Contemplation and Compassion

Many fear that contemplative life separates us from the world. Yet true contemplation gives birth to deep compassion. When we no longer see through the eyes of the ego but through divine awareness, the suffering of others is no longer foreign. Their pain resonates in our own heart. Contemplation does not numb sensitivity — it refines it.

This compassion is not burden, but grace. Not pity, but communion. Not entanglement, but resonance. God does not watch from outside — He suffers and heals with us. And whoever lives in God's awareness is not passive, but participates in the redemption of the world — through quiet presence, even without words.

Silent Action: The Work of the Spirit Within

The purest action is that which does not serve the self but flows from God. It is not loud, not meant to impress, but simple, natural, and deep. A glance, a silence, a gentle gesture can be sacred when it arises from presence. This is the work of the Spirit: transforming the ordinary into the eternal.

The contemplative person is not inactive — they are free. No longer driven by the ego's will, but moved by the call of the Spirit. Thus, work, relationship, service, teaching, and even silence can become the work of God. It is not we who act, but the One who lives within us. This is not metaphor, but reality: the Son within the Father, dwelling also in us.

Practice – Recognizing the Movements of Love

Choose a simple daily action — washing dishes, speaking with someone, walking, or offering help. Before you begin, pause and silently say: *"Let this be an act of love."*

Then be fully present. Notice how the movement is not yours — it flows through you. Watch how the simple becomes sacred.

This practice helps you realize: love is the movement of God within us.

24

True Help – The Art of Compassionate Presence

True Help – The Art of Compassionate Presence

True help is not telling another what to do, but being fully present with them in what they are living through.

Jesus helped in this way: He did not merely teach — He *saw*, He *heard*, and He *felt* the hearts of those before Him.

Those who came to Him did not only receive guidance but the holding Presence in which their souls rediscovered their own strength.

This is the quiet form of love — *attention.*

When someone is in pain, they rarely need advice; they long to be *truly heard.*

Not half-heartedly, not superficially, but with deep and open-hearted listening.

For when we are truly heard without judgment, our souls breathe again — loneliness dissolves, and light begins to enter where pain once ruled.

This attentive presence *is* the practice of compassion.

In genuine attention, there is no haste and no urge to fix.

If someone cries — let them cry.

If they are afraid — let them speak their fear.

If they are angry — allow it to be expressed.

We do not need to "make it better," for often the greatest help is not solving, but *holding* — offering space where the other can simply *be*.

Love is not always action; sometimes it is *presence*.

Many who try to help are unconsciously soothing their own discomfort.

They cannot bear another's pain, so they rush to reassure — "It's not so bad," or "Don't think about it."

But even well-meant words like these send the message: *You shouldn't feel what you feel.*

And the soul retreats, hiding its pain in shame and suppression.

Loving help, by contrast, gives space.

It says: *"I'm here. You can feel. I understand."*

It does not take the pain away — it stays beside it, allowing the other to find their own way out.

True healing never comes from outside; it arises from within — but it needs a safe space where one dares to feel and to see clearly again.

If we wish to help, we must learn to listen in a way that opens the other's heart.

Do not correct, analyze, or rush to respond.

Be with them first — only later, if they ask, offer a suggestion.

Real guidance does not come from the mind, but from the quiet understanding that appears when two souls are in tune.

The wise helper does not fix another's life — they kindle a light within it, so that the person may see their own next step.

When you are present in this way, you become an instrument of God's Presence.

Jesus, too, did not always speak — sometimes He simply *looked* — and in that gaze, there was fullness.

He did not hurry or force — He loved.

Whoever listens with such a heart is already healing, even without words.

This is true help:

Not intervention, but *being-with*.

Not solution, but *listening*.

Not control, but *trust* — trust that the same light lives within the other, capable of guiding them home.

When we help in this way, we no longer act from our own will, but let love flow through us.

And this love does not tire, for it does not come from us.

It is the Presence of which Jesus said:

"Whoever abides in Me and I in him bears much fruit." (John 15:5)

True help, then, is becoming a conscious channel of God's love — to listen, to understand, to give space, and to allow the light of awareness to arise in the other's heart.

In such moments, conversation becomes prayer, and compassion becomes healing.

Practical Guide to Compassionate Conversation

1. Be fully present.

Turn toward the other person in body and spirit.

Do not plan what to say next or seek immediate solutions.

Your attention itself is healing.

Let them feel that what they say truly matters.

2. Accept their feelings — don't evaluate them.

Avoid phrases like "It's not that bad" or "Others have it worse."

Instead, say:

"I understand this is hard for you."

"I can see this is painful."

"What you're saying matters."

Simple words, but they create space — and space brings relief.

3. Reflect what you hear.

Gently summarize to show you've understood:

"You feel disappointed because you weren't heard."

"If I understand correctly, you need safety more than advice right now."

Reflection helps them see their feelings more clearly — and feel less alone.

4. Do not rush the silence.

Silence is not empty — it is the sacred space where truth matures.

Do not fill it too quickly.

Often, the deepest insights are born in silence.

5. Offer advice only if asked.

True help is not telling them what to do but helping them find their own way.

If you share an idea, begin softly:

"I may be wrong, but something came to mind..."

"Do you think it might help if...?"

This keeps their freedom intact and invites, rather than pressures.

6. Offer safety, not solutions.

You don't need all the answers.

You don't need to make it "better."

Just don't be afraid of their pain.

Loving presence doesn't change feelings by force — it allows them to transform naturally.

This is the essence of compassionate listening: not seeking to improve, but to *understand.*

When we listen this way, conversation becomes more than words — it becomes sacred space.

A place where the soul can rest and rediscover its own inner light.

For true help lies not in what we *say*, but in how we *are present.*

This is the way of Jesus: the way of silence, attention, and love —

where healing happens not through effort, but through Presence.

25

The Sanctification of Suffering – God's Light in the Fractures

Suffering Is Not the Absence of the Divine Presence

Many believe that when we suffer, God disappears — that pain is the failure of faith. Yet suffering is not the absence of the Divine Presence, but its deepest possibility. The Cross does not mean that God abandoned humanity, but that God entered human pain. Jesus did not lose His divine connection upon the Cross — it was there that it reached its fullness. Whatever form it takes, suffering does not exclude God; it opens the heart to recognize Him precisely where we least expected to find Him.

God does not avoid us in our hours of suffering — He is there, in the very center of our pain. Presence is not always radiant or joyful; at times it feels more like a quiet strength that holds us when we can no longer hold ourselves. In suffering, nothing new begins — rather, the old becomes transparent: the Spirit has never left us.

The Vastness of the Broken Heart

Pain not only wounds, it opens. The broken heart is not weak — it is open. God does not choose perfect forms, but cracked vessels, because through them His light shines most freely. Just as darkness reveals the flame of a candle, so suffering reveals the depth of Presence.

In suffering, the heart softens. We lose the illusion of control and open to what is greater than ourselves. Often after deep pain, a person begins to see differently — more clearly, more gently, more deeply. This is not because pain is "good," but because when we remain present within it, God transforms it.

The broken heart is like a window the Spirit has opened. Where once we built walls, pain brings them down. And where once we stood alone, the Infinite enters. The silence of a broken heart is often deeper than the noise of happiness — for there, we no longer seek, we simply behold. And in that stillness, God is born within us anew.

Listening Within Pain

In suffering, attention naturally turns inward. The body, emotions, and memories all intensify. Yet here lies the opportunity: if we can remain present in pain without rejecting it, something changes. Pain becomes not only anguish but a call — a call back to God. Pain asks, *"Where are You?"* And attention answers, *"Here You are."*

This does not mean we must seek suffering. God does not desire pain — He desires wholeness. Only that when it appears, we do not flee from it. We do not close off, but allow the Spirit to permeate and transform it. At the threshold of pain, God waits — not to erase it, but to be with us in it. And in that presence, something new begins: not the end of pain, but the birth of love within it.

Suffering as a Sacred Fire

In the Christian mystical tradition, suffering is often understood through the image of sacrifice — not as self-punishment, but as offering. When we bring our pain before God rather than hiding it, it is no longer merely ours. It becomes a small thread woven into the redemption of the world. Just as Christ's crucifixion was not in vain, our smaller crosses too are woven into the fabric of divine love.

In this fire, the human being is not destroyed, but purified. Emerging from suffering, the soul often discovers a peace deeper than ever before — a peace that no longer depends on circumstances, but flows directly from God.

Practice – Presence in Pain

Sit quietly. Bring your attention to an area of tension, anxiety, or pain. Do not try to change it — simply stay with it. Observe the bodily sensation: where is it? what shape, movement, or temperature does it have? Watch it as if you were with God in that very place. Silently say, *"I am here. And You are here."*

Breathe into the sensation. No need to analyze — just be present. If tears come, let them. If emptiness arises, rest in it. This presence is not weakness, but holiness. Pain is the cross upon which God appeared — so that even there, we might be with Him.

Remain like this for a few minutes. And when you finish, whisper softly: *"Thy will be done — even in this."*

26

The Ways of the Ego

Trapthe Modes of the Mind
The human mind is like a delicate and intricate mechanism,
capable of operating on three distinct levels.

These can be called: **the mode of habit, the mode of control,** and **the mode of presence.**

All three arise from the same source — the light of consciousness — yet depending on our level of awareness, they lead our lives in completely different directions.

1. The Mode of Habit

In this mode, the mind acts almost automatically. Thoughts, emotions, and behaviors link together through an invisible chain of conditioning, without real awareness being present.

We experience this as an **autopilot state:** we drive, eat, talk — yet we are not truly *here*.

Our soul seems to drift elsewhere, and life passes before us like a dream.

In this state, consciousness falls asleep, and the ego — the system of habits, fears, and automatic reactions — takes control.

We lose touch with the living moment, and only later do we realize that we were not truly alive.

In the habitual mode, the body is tense, the breath shallow, and the mind loops through repetitive thoughts, as if the same melody kept spinning on an old record.

Here we do not *live* but merely *survive*.

The purpose of practice is to gently awaken from this automatic state — to pause and ask:

"What is happening within me right now?"

That moment of recognition is the first spark of awakening.

2. The Mode of the Over-Controlled Mind

In this mode, the mind constantly searches for problems and tries to fix them.

The ego appears here as the planner, the strategist, the thinker.

Two invisible axes drive this activity:

1. "How can I get from where I am to where I want to be?"
2. "How can I avoid what I fear or wish to escape?"

These two forces shape most human decisions.

The mind continually compares: *Where am I now? Where should I be? What must I do to get there?*

This mode can be powerful and useful for practical matters — but when it dominates every aspect of life, it becomes exhausting.

We are constantly striving, improving, avoiding, chasing.

This is the **voice of the ego** — the inner controller that is never satisfied.

The paradox is that the more the current moment resembles what the mind wants to avoid, the stronger fear and anxiety become.

The mental engine overheats, the body tightens, the breath shortens, and the present fades behind the horizon of the goal.

Escaping this mode does not mean stopping all action, but **noticing when the mind has taken over**.

It becomes especially problematic when *inner experiences* — thoughts and feelings — turn into "problems" to fix or escape from.

The mind then tries to suppress, change, or avoid its own content, which only strengthens it, creating a **vicious circle** of tension and suffering.

The way out is **mindful awareness** — meeting inner experience with openness and compassion.

We give attention to what is, allowing it to exist without forcing change.

When the mind pulls us back into control, we can always return: observe, allow, release, and redirect our focus to the now — to the breath, bodily sensations, or a sound around us.

Thoughts and emotions are not enemies.

They are not facts or absolute truths — only inner stories, echoes of the past.

When we see them in this light, they lose their power.

We do not fight them; we simply recognize which of the three modes we are in, name it, see it, and return to presence.

This is how the circle dissolves and the healing space of awareness opens.

The mind keeps three things in constant view:

1. What I want to achieve.
2. How far I am from it.
3. What I must avoid.

These arise as **words and sentences (thoughts)**, **images (mental pictures)**, and finally as **feelings (bodily sensations)**.

3. The Mode of Presence

This is the natural state of consciousness.

Here, **perception is primary, judgment secondary**.

We do not try to reach or avoid anything — we simply *observe*.

When we allow experience itself to be the teacher — observing thoughts, feelings, and bodily sensations with openness, acceptance, and love — we shift into this sacred space.

In this field there is no struggle, no judgment, only pure, gentle attention.

And in that attention — it is truly **God seeing Himself**.

For this awareness *is* the Spirit alive within all things.

The mode of presence is not a trance, but our most natural way of being, from which the noise of the ego distracts us.

The key is noticing — seeing when the mind tries to control, and acknowledging it without judgment.

The moment you see it, you have already shifted.

Presence is not effort, but **surrender**.

Not achievement, but **openness**.

In this state, every thought, feeling, and sensation appears like a wave upon the vast ocean — arising and dissolving, while the depth remains unmoved.

Every practice serves this subtle transition.

Every moment of awareness is a step into the light of the Soul.

When this recognition dawns, the ego ceases to be the enemy and becomes the teacher — showing us when we are not yet present.

And this recognition leads to true freedom.

For when we learn to live from presence, the mind becomes a quiet servant, and the **Light of God** — the Soul itself — guides our life.

This section is not a conclusion but a deepening — an exploration of the workings of consciousness and the soul before the book turns toward its final revelations.

Previous chapters spoke of the purification of the heart, the awakening of love and presence; now we look into the roots of what veils that light.

The mind is not sinful — it is a seeker, trying in its limited way to understand life.

When the light of the Spirit shines through it, the mind too finds peace: fear becomes understanding, resistance becomes acceptance, and separation dissolves into unity.

Darkness has no existence of its own — it is only the absence of light.

And the ego's patterns are not "evil" — merely unconscious movements lacking light.

Once you see them, you are no longer one with them: **the very seeing is the beginning of liberation.**

The Mind as a Fabric of Illusion

The natural function of the mind is to distinguish, to give form, to seek order — thus supporting survival and understanding.

Since ancient times, it has been the tool by which humanity has navigated the world: recognizing patterns, perceiving danger, seeking connection.

But as the mind grew stronger, attention narrowed more and more into the realm of thought.

Thus the *story* is born — the woven fabric of the mind in which we interpret ourselves and others:

Who am I? Who are they? What threatens me, and what keeps me safe?

This story seems to organize life, yet it often imprisons it.

What we believe, we begin to see — and our seeing confirms our belief.

The mind strengthens itself, circling endlessly, maintaining the illusion of a personal world.

In contrast, the **Christ Light within us** is not a story but *presence* —

the field of pure vision, where things are not judged but revealed as movements of the Spirit.

In this light, the mind falls silent, and separation gives way to understanding; fear transforms into trust.

Here, seeing no longer casts shadows but returns to the Source from which every thought arises.

Practical key:

Whenever you notice that a story begins to "pull you in" — through rumination, blame, or self-defense — silently say to yourself:

"This is a story. It is not reality. I return to experience."

Then gently return to the sensations of the body and the rhythm of the breath.

The Role of the Ego on the Path of the Soul – Not an Enemy, but a Misunderstood Servant

The ego is a system tuned for survival — it seeks to protect what it believes to be "me" through the illusions of separation and control.

Throughout human history, this force has helped us distinguish, decide, and set boundaries — yet at the same time, it has also closed us off from our Source.

The ego is not evil; it is simply **misunderstood**. It fears dissolution, thinking it means death, when in truth it is the **doorway to freedom**.

The problem is not that the ego exists, but that we mistake ourselves for it.

Through identification with the ego, we confine ourselves within narrower limits — roles, past experiences, opinions, and fears.

When the ego leads, perception contracts: the world appears dangerous, and others seem threatening.

But when the **Soul leads**, the heart expands — understanding, forgiveness, and compassion begin to flow.

In the eyes of the Soul, the ego is not an enemy but a **child afraid of the dark**, longing only for light.

When consciousness looks upon it with love, the ego too finds peace:

defensiveness turns into humility, fear becomes trust, and the need to possess transforms into the joy of sharing.

It is essential to understand that the ego is not to be destroyed or suppressed.

The more we fight it, the stronger it becomes — for attention is its food.

The ego can be **softened** through presence, patience, and compassion — just as fear can only dissolve in light.

In meditation and in conscious living, the ego no longer rules but becomes a **co-worker** of the Soul.

It is given tasks through which it can serve, aligning its energy with the intentions of love.

When we learn to invite cooperation instead of conflict, the ego steps into service of the divine purpose.

Turning phrase:

> *"The ego doesn't need to disappear — it just isn't the driver anymore.*
> *I hand the wheel over to Presence."*

The Origin and Dynamics of Patterns – A Map to the Shadow

All inner patterns arise from the same root: **the belief in fear and lack**.

Each pattern carries with it a trigger, an automatic thought, a bodily sensation, and a behavioral response.

The aim is not self-criticism, but **illumination** — allowing light to shine upon what was unconscious, observing it in presence, with acceptance and without judgment.

Pattern-Inquiry Questions:

- What triggered it?
- What thought appeared?
- Where do I feel it in the body?
- What emotion does it manifest as?

Through this gentle investigation, the hidden movements of the shadow reveal themselves — not to be fought, but to be **understood and embraced in awareness.**

27

Patterns of the Mind

Fear (Anxiety, Control)

Core Belief: "I am not safe."

Automatic Reaction: Scanning the future, catastrophizing, overusing control.

Body: Tightness in the chest, knot in the stomach, accelerated or shallow breathing.

Practice: Observe the natural rhythm of your breath, and when the mind starts weaving stories, gently return to the sensations of the body. Allow the fear to be felt *as it is.*

Christ Vision: "Peace I leave with you; my peace I give to you."

Peace is not found in circumstances, but in Presence.

The Nature of Fear

Fear is one of humanity's oldest emotions.

Its root does not lie in the present, but in the mind's *projections of the future.*

Fear always assumes that something bad is coming and that *this moment is not enough.*

It arises from the belief that safety lives in external situations, events, or people — not within us.

Yet in truth, safety is not a condition; **it is Presence.**

The awareness that perceives fear remains untouched by it.

How to Recognize It

The body subtly signals whenever the mind senses danger:
the chest tightens, the stomach contracts, the breath quickens or halts.
Perception narrows — everything orbits around the threat.

Thoughts then begin crafting future scenarios, and consciousness shifts from reality into an imagined story.

Here begins the circle of fear: **feeling → thought → story.**

The Turning Point

The release of fear does not come from running away, but from *allowing it fully.*

Presence does not fight — it *sees.*

When we allow fear to exist without feeding its thoughts, it gradually transforms: it becomes a raw sensation, and then dissolves into stillness.

The awareness that remains is stronger than any fear.

Practices

1. Three Exhales of Homecoming

Close your eyes. Let your shoulders drop.

Take three long, slow exhalations.

With each breath out, release what you cannot control.

Notice how quickly the body responds to Presence.

2. Sole Anchor

Bring your attention to the soles of your feet.

Feel their contact with the ground.

Silently repeat: "Here."

The body is always in the present; returning to it means returning to reality.

3. The Fear Interview

Ask yourself:

What is actually happening right now?
And what exists only in my imagination?
Distinguishing between the two is already the beginning of freedom.

Shift in Vision

Safety does not depend on favorable circumstances.

The world changes, but the essence that perceives it is unchanging.

Peace arises where awareness is awake.

Fear rules only as long as you believe you *are* it.

The moment you see that what appears in your mind is **not reality**, tension begins to release.

Always remember:

The goal is **allowance**, not control —

not to change thoughts or feelings, but to let them be bathed in the light of awareness.

Anger (Emotion, Attack/Defense)

Core Belief: "Something is unjust; my boundaries are in danger."

Automatic Reaction: Blaming, moralizing, showing force.

Body: Heat waves, clenched fists, tense shoulders.

Practice: Recognize the anger, allow it to be present, observe it in the body, and soften it through gentle awareness.

Christ Perspective: Behind anger, there is always a wound. Love is not weakness — it sees through error and draws boundaries softly yet firmly.

The Deeper Nature of Anger

Many misunderstand anger, as if it were a sin in itself. Yet when it arises from a pure source, anger is one of the deepest expressions of love.

Anger becomes destructive only when it is driven by selfishness, fear, or wounded pride — but when it arises in defense of truth and divine order, it is a **movement of the Soul.**

Jesus Himself showed that love is not always gentle. When He entered the temple in Jerusalem and saw it turned into a marketplace, He said:

> *"My house shall be called a house of prayer, but you have made it a den of thieves."*
> (Matthew 21:13)

*Then He overturned the tables of the money changers and drove out
those who profaned the sacred space.*

*This was not the anger of hatred, but the **anger of divine truth** — the
flame of Love that purifies all that distorts the holy.*

Such anger does not destroy; it **restores.**

It does not seek to harm others but protects the purity of the Spirit.

This is not the ego's reaction, but the heartbeat of the Divine, refusing to
let the sacred be defiled.

When anger is born in the heart of love, it becomes the **judgment of
heavenly light upon darkness.**

Those who know this inner flame understand that it is not hatred that
speaks, but Love itself — unwilling to compromise with injustice.

Recognizing Anger

The body quickly reveals its presence: waves of heat, clenched fists, tight
shoulders, rapid breathing.

Thoughts arise as blame, moral judgment, or a search for righteousness.

Yet behind these lies a deeper message — the heart is defending itself.

Anger points to where love or safety feels missing.

The Turning Point

The recognition of anger is the key to presence.

When you pause instead of reacting, and simply feel the energy within the
body, **the fire turns into light.**

In the gentle presence of awareness, anger reveals what it is trying to
protect — often self-worth, sometimes a wish to avoid suffering.

When this is understood, anger loses its destructive force and transforms
into **creative energy:** clarity, honesty, and loving boundary-setting.

Practices

1. Observing Anger in Real Time

When anger arises, do not suppress it or act on it immediately.

Stay with it for a few breaths.

Notice where it lives in the body.

Awareness illuminates the feeling, and its deeper message slowly unfolds.

2. The Love Beneath It

Ask yourself: *"What is this anger protecting in me? What love or value is it trying to guard?"*

When the answer appears, tension often begins to soften.

3. Transforming Anger Constructively

If action is needed, use the energy of understood anger for clear and honest communication.

Instead of attacking the other person — which only makes them close off — express your truth gently:

> *"When this happens, I feel tension, and I would appreciate if…"*
> *Such boundaries are drawn from love, not separation.*

Shift in Vision

Anger is not your enemy but a **signal light** pointing toward wounded love.

When you learn to meet it with awareness, it no longer chains you — it guides you.

It shows where clarity, expression, or release is needed.

To see in this way is to stop fighting and to begin **aligning with the heart's truth.**

Envy (Comparison, Sense of Lack)

Core Belief: "Another's abundance is my lack."

Automatic Reaction: Comparison, self-devaluation, cynicism.

Body: Constricted chest, lump in the throat.

Antidote: *Mudita* — joy in the goodness of another.

Practice: *"The Light of Envy"* — conscious blessing:

> *"May you be blessed, and may what blooms in you also open within me."*

The Subtle Nature of Envy

Envy is a subtle yet deeply influential emotion.

It arises when we see another's goodness, success, or joy — and something within the heart tightens, as if their light diminished our own.

But this feeling is not about the other person; it reflects an inner sense of lack — the belief that *there is not enough*, that *we have been left out.*

This belief is what separates us from the natural abundance that has always been within us.

How to Recognize It

The body quickly signals the shadow of envy: constriction in the chest, a knot in the throat, subtle tension around the heart.

Meanwhile, the mind begins to measure and compare:

"They succeed so easily..."
"I'll never reach that..."

In that moment, attention loses touch with what already *is*, and projects the illusion of lack.

Yet this is precisely the moment of potential awakening — the chance to see that the pain is nothing other than *forgotten love.*

The Turning Point

Envy is not an enemy but a **teacher.**

When you consciously observe it — neither pushing it away nor feeding it — the heart slowly reopens.

You begin to see that what you admire in another also lives within you, only dormant.

The abundance of others takes nothing from you; it reminds you of what is possible.

When this realization dawns, scarcity dissolves, and the heart awakens to its natural joy.

- **Practices**
  ### 1. The Light of Envy
  When envy arises, pause and say silently: *"This is the heart's contraction."*
  Take a deep breath and bring the light of awareness into the feeling.
  Allow envy to exist within the space of presence — do not push it away.
  As you stay, you begin to see: the goodness you perceive in the other is not "out there" — it is also alive in you.
  ### 2. Conscious Blessing
  Look toward the person you once envied and say inwardly:

  "May you be blessed, and may what blooms in you also open within me."
  This simple inner prayer transforms the energy of envy into gratitude and inspiration.

3. Vision of Abundance
Write down three things you are grateful for today — not just objects, but moments, connections, or feelings.

Gratitude retunes the mind to abundance and dissolves the illusion of lack.

Shift in Vision

Abundance is not the accumulation of possessions, but the natural state of being.

To see another's light is already to be *in* the light — otherwise you could not see it.

Thus envy becomes a **gate of awakening:** the realization that every goodness you perceive already dwells within you.

To rejoice in another's joy is to step into the current of love.

From this recognition, envy transforms into **motivation and inspiration** — the impulse to unfold your own gifts while appreciating the blessings that are already yours.

Shame (Sense of Deficiency in Self-Worth)

Core Belief: "Something is wrong with me."
Automatic Reaction: Hiding, people-pleasing, self-punishment.
Body: Blushing, collapsed posture, tightness in the stomach.
Practice: *Naming the emotion* and *self-directed compassion* — place a hand on your chest, exhale slowly, and speak gently within:

> *"Suffering is present; I am not alone."*
> ***View of Grace:*** *Existence itself is inherently valuable.*

The Deep Misperception

Shame is one of the deepest human emotions — it separates us from ourselves and from others.

Its root is the belief that something within us is fundamentally flawed or unlovable.

This belief seeps into our sense of self and begins to shape behavior: we strive to please, we hide, we punish ourselves.

Shame is the feeling of disconnection — the moment we forget that we are loved **exactly as we are.**

How to Recognize It

When shame arises, the body contracts: the face flushes, the posture sinks, the stomach tightens.

The gaze lowers, the chest closes.

An inner voice accuses:

> *"You're not good enough."*
> *"Others are better than you."*
> *"If they really knew you, they wouldn't love you."*

In that moment, body and mind close off the heart from the inner ray of light that has always been there.

The Turning Point

Healing shame is not a fight, but an act of gentle presence.

If you stop running from it and allow it to be felt, you will notice: beneath shame always lies **love** — the longing to connect, to be accepted.

When you allow this feeling and look upon it with kindness, shame slowly dissolves in the warmth of compassion.

The heart remembers: *there was never anything wrong with you — you only believed you didn't belong to love.*

Practices

1. Naming and Compassion

Place your hand on your chest, take a deep breath, and say silently:

"Suffering is present. I am not alone. I can be gentle with myself."
Notice how the body begins to relax.
The warmth of your hand is the heart's message: I am still here.

2. Mirror Practice

Look into the mirror and seek the child in your eyes who only ever wanted love.

Say to them:

"I see you, and you are enough as you are."
This simple sentence rebuilds inner trust.

3. Act of Self-Love

During the day, choose one small act of kindness toward yourself — rest, a quiet walk, or a kind word.

Each of these moments softens the wall of shame.

Shift in Vision

In place of shame, gratitude begins to bloom.

You recognize how much you already have — your breath, your life, your capacity to learn.

Self-worth grows not from perfection, but from valuing the goodness already within you.

Thus shame transforms into **motivation — not to prove, but to love.**

Your very existence is sacred, and from that realization, true self-respect is born.

The Need to Please / "People-Pleasing"

Core Belief: "My lovability is conditional."

Automatic Reaction: Saying yes almost always; blurred or nonexistent personal boundaries.

Body: Tension in the neck and shoulders, fatigue.

Practice: *"I say no with love"* script; values-based decision list (*What truly matters?*).

Christ Example: Love of truth is not the same as constant approval.

The Deep Misperception

The need to please is a **misunderstood form of seeking love.**

When we believe we are worthy of acceptance only if we satisfy others, we forget that **real love is not earned — it is given.**

This belief leads us to say "yes" when our heart feels "no."

Attention turns outward: *What do they think of me? What must I do to be loved?*

Slowly, our own voice fades, and the soul grows weary.

How to Recognize It

The body speaks first: the shoulders and neck tighten, the chest feels heavy, fatigue becomes constant.

Thoughts revolve around:

"If I say no, I'll hurt them."
"I don't want to disappoint anyone."
"They need to like me."

These thoughts are born not from love, but from **fear** — the fear of rejection if we dare to be ourselves.

The Turning Point

The moment of truth arrives when you realize: **real love never demands dishonesty.**

When you always say yes while feeling no inside, you are not protecting the other — you are sacrificing the truth of the relationship.

Love has room for boundaries.

The heart not only receives — it also guides.

To say "no" gently yet sincerely is not rejection — it is an act of alignment with your soul.

Practices

1. "I Say No with Love" Script

When you feel the impulse to say yes automatically, pause and breathe.
Silently say:

> *"With love, I say no."*
> *Feel how love flows not from pleasing others, but from truth itself.*

2. Values-Based Decision List

Write down what truly matters to you.
Before each decision, ask:

> *"Is this aligned with who I am?"*
> *If not, a "yes" would only be born from fear.*

3. Listening to the Body's Signals

Before agreeing to something, check in with your body.
Do your shoulders tighten? Does your stomach clench?
These are the body's quiet ways of saying, *"This yes is not true."*
Shift in Vision
True connection does not require constant approval.
The **love of truth** is not obedience.
Jesus Himself spoke from love, not fear — His boundaries were gentle yet

firm.

Those who live this way no longer obey others' expectations but the **truth within.**

Love does not demand perfection — only **honesty.**

Possession / Attachment

Core Belief: "If I let go, I will lose."

Automatic Reaction: Control, jealousy, delayed release.

Body: Tension in the lower abdomen, holding of breath.

Practice: *Breath of Surrender* — with each exhale, say silently:

"Thy will be done."

Deep Misperception: "If I let go, I will lose."

The Nature of Attachment

Possession and attachment are subtle forms of fear.

We believe that if we release what matters to us — a person, a situation, an object, or even a story from the past — emptiness will remain.

The mind therefore tries to grasp what is, by its nature, ever-changing.

Yet everything we cling to slowly distances us from what we truly seek: **peace.**

Letting go is not loss, but a **return** to what never left — the trust within.

How to Recognize It

The body immediately reveals when you are holding on: tension in the lower abdomen, restrained breathing, a sense of inner tightness.

The mind circles around the same questions:

"What will happen if I let go?"
"I couldn't bear to lose this."

Fear arises from losing control — from the idea that life cannot flow without our interference.

But the moment you see this, the breath deepens, and the grip begins to soften.

The Turning Point

The true turning point is the realization that **you don't need to hold on to keep what is yours.**

What truly belongs to you can never be lost.

When possession gives way to trust, relationships do not weaken — they **purify.**

Letting go is not indifference, but a deeper form of love: allowing everything and everyone to unfold in their own divine order.

Freedom is not found in distance, but in the absence of clinging.

Practices

1. Breath of Surrender

Sit comfortably and observe your breathing.

With every exhale, whisper within:

"Thy will be done."
Feel the body soften, the tension release.
Each breath reminds you that after every exhale, a new inhale arrives
— life always continues.

2. Allowance Meditation

Bring to mind a situation or person you struggle to release.

Breathe into the feeling and say:

"I allow this, too, to be part of life."
Do not try to change it — simply witness what is.
Acceptance opens the heart.

3. Gratitude for the Passing

Write down three things you let go of today — even small ones: a thought, an expectation, a resentment.

Next to each, note what you received in return — lightness, peace, space. This teaches the mind that letting go does not take — it **gives.**

Shift in Vision

Letting go is not the opposite of love — it is its **highest form.**

Only those who trust can truly love.

Attachment is the movement of the controlling mind; release is the movement of the trusting heart.

When you surrender to what is greater than yourself, you do not lose — you **unite** with the flowing life itself.

Love does not possess — it simply *is present.*

Rumination and Catastrophizing

Core Belief: "If I think enough, I'll solve it."

Automatic Reaction: Repetitive mental loops, story-spinning.

Body: Tension in the forehead, clenched jaw, overall bodily tension and anxiety — a subtle sign of avoidance.

Deep Misperception: "If I think enough, I'll solve it."

The Nature of Rumination

Rumination is one of the mind's most persistent movements.

It is as if consciousness constantly tries to **fix the past** or **prevent the future.**

The intention is not wrong — it seeks safety — yet excessive thinking steals the very peace it was trying to find.

The mind circles endlessly, while the simple, living experience of the present fades from awareness.

How to Recognize It

The body often knows before the mind:

tension around the forehead, jaw tightness, stiff shoulders, subtle restlessness throughout the body.

Breathing becomes shallow, and attention contracts into the head.

Thoughts begin to repeat familiar phrases:

"What if I had...?"
  "What will happen if...?"
  "I shouldn't have..."

This spiral doesn't solve — it sustains.

The Turning Point

The shift comes when you realize that **thinking does not always lead to understanding.**

Presence is not the absence of thought, but the **restoration of connection** to what is here now.

Redirecting attention to the body, to the breath, or to sensory experience interrupts the automatic mental loop.

Solutions no longer arise from overthinking, but from the **clarity of direct awareness.**

Practices

You may combine these with any of the **Meditation Practices** described earlier.

1. Three-Breath Return

When you notice you're caught in a thought loop, pause and take three slow, conscious breaths.

With each exhale, allow the body to rest and silently say:

"I am here now."

2. Body-Sensation Anchor

Shift attention to a bodily sensation — the soles of your feet touching the ground, or the rise and fall of your chest as you breathe.

Each time a thought pulls you away, return here.

The goal is not to change thoughts, but to **change your relationship** with them.

3. Thought as Cloud

Imagine your thoughts as clouds drifting across the sky.

You are not the clouds — you are the sky that sees them.

This image softens the belief that every thought is true or important.

4. Question the Thought

When a thought keeps returning, ask:

> *"Is this useful right now?"*
> *If not, smile gently at it and come back to the present.*
> *This question breaks the automatic identification with thought.*

5. Recognize, Allow, Redirect

When you catch yourself ruminating, name it: *"rumination."*

Acknowledge its presence without judgment.

Then gently redirect attention to a current, tangible activity — even something small or ordinary.

If the thought returns, simply repeat the same sequence.

Shift in Vision

Behind rumination always lies the **search for safety.**

But real safety does not live in control — it lives in **trust.**

When you allow things to be as they are, without needing to figure out everything, the mind begins to rest.

Wisdom is born not in thought, but in the **clarity of awareness.**

Then thinking becomes no longer a whirlpool but a tool — **your servant, not your master.**

Avoidance

Core Belief: "I can't handle it — something bad will happen."

Automatic Reaction: Procrastination, screen-escape, overeating.

Body: Sense of emptiness, dullness, anxiety, or tension in various areas — especially the forehead, shoulders, lower back, arms, and legs.

Deep Misperception: "I can't handle it — something bad will happen."

The Nature of Avoidance

Avoidance is a quiet form of fear.

We believe that if we don't look at something, we won't have to feel the pain that comes with it.

The mind tries to protect us from what it deems *too much to bear.*

But everything we avoid continues to grow in the background, returning again and again.

Through **mindful presence**, we learn that difficult feelings are not enemies but passing experiences — and that they *can* be borne when we stop trying to change them.

How to Recognize It

In the body, avoidance often appears as dullness or anxiety.

There may be tightness in the forehead, shoulders, lower back, arms, or legs.

A sense of heaviness, emptiness, or disconnection may arise.

In behavior, it may look like procrastination, overeating, scrolling screens, or overactivity — anything that distracts from the present moment.

The common thread: attention shifts away from what *is*, toward something that promises temporary relief.

The Turning Point

Healing begins the moment you stop running.

Feelings do not need to be suppressed or controlled — only **noticed** as they arise and pass.

When discomfort appears, try not to look away.

Allow it to be there and observe it in the body as if it were a wave — rising, cresting, and subsiding on its own.

In this seeing, fear loses its power, and you discover **inner stability.**

Practices

1. Three-Step Presence

1 *Pause* — Notice what is happening within you right now: thought, emotion, bodily sensation.

2 *Breathe* — Take one or two conscious breaths, feeling the movement of

air.

3 *Expand Awareness* — Include the whole body and your surroundings, allowing everything to be just as it is.

This short practice interrupts the automatic flight response.

2. Body Sensation Allowance

When you sense avoidance or procrastination, bring attention back into the body.

Locate the area of tension and breathe gently into it.

Don't try to dissolve it — simply hold it in awareness.

Attention itself heals.

3. Conscious Action

Choose one small thing you usually avoid — a message, a task, a conversation.

Do it today, in mindful presence.

Notice how anxiety lessens in the very act of doing.

Avoidance feels hardest only *before* we step into presence.

Shift in Vision

Behind avoidance lies the belief: **"I can't handle this."**

Yet experience always reveals the opposite — you *can.*

Pain can be observed, felt, and ultimately released.

Mindful presence does not take away your strength — it *returns* it.

It teaches you to trust that whatever comes, you can endure it.

Peace is not the absence of difficulty, but the **ability to stay with it in awareness.**

Perfectionism / Rigid Control

Core Belief: "Only the flawless is valuable."

Automatic Reaction: Micromanagement, self-criticism.

Body: Shoulder and back tension, shallow breathing.

Antidote: *"Good enough in love."* — a values-based focus on connection, not on flawless form.

Deep Misperception: "Only the flawless is valuable."

The Nature of Perfectionism

Perfectionism is born from a lack of self-acceptance.

We believe that if we fix every mistake — if we are good enough, precise enough, disciplined enough — we will finally feel safe and lovable.

But this belief makes love conditional and sacrifices the joy of the present moment for the illusion of perfection.

Control does not lead to peace; it leads to rigidity.

Love begins where we allow ourselves to be human — imperfect, yet whole.

How to Recognize It

Under perfectionism, the body stays in constant alert: shoulders and back tight, breath shallow, attention narrowed.

Thoughts search for flaws, re-evaluate the past, and worry about the future.

The inner voice says:

"I could have done better."
"This isn't enough."

Such inner severity closes the heart's softness and drains the body's vitality.

The Turning Point

The shift comes when you realize: **you don't need to be perfect to be worthy.**

Mindful awareness teaches you to see mistakes not as failures but as information.

When you notice the impulse toward perfection, don't judge it — simply observe how it feels in the body.

Each time you allow something to be *"good enough,"* you take one step closer to peace.

Practices

1. "Good Enough in Love" Practice

Choose a situation where you tend to over-strive for perfection.

Ask yourself:

"Is this good enough for love?"
   If the answer is yes, release the remaining tension.
   Life is not flawless — it is alive.

2. Conscious Imperfection

Do something intentionally *not* perfect — leave a detail unfinished, resist correcting something minor.

Observe what happens in your body.

The goal is not carelessness, but freedom from the tyranny of control.

3. Values-Based Focus

When making a decision, look not at the form but at the value:

"Does this bring me closer to connection, love, and what truly matters?"
   In doing so, attention shifts from the flaw to the heart.

Shift in Vision

The pursuit of perfection is the path of fear; acceptance of the present is the path of love.

Flawless form is only a momentary illusion, but the connection born from the heart is eternal.

When you allow something to be *"good enough,"* you are really saying, *"I am enough."*

True strength lies not in control, but in **trust** — the trust that life itself moves toward harmony when we stop over-managing it.

Scarcity Schema

Core Belief: "There is not enough (time, money, love, attention)."

Automatic Reaction: Hoarding, envy, rushing.

Antidote: *Gratitude practice* and *small acts of giving* — practicing abundance by noticing what already exists.

Deep Misperception: "There is not enough (time, money, love, attention)."
The Nature of the Scarcity Mindset

The scarcity schema arises from a **consciousness of lack** — the belief that life's resources are limited and that there is always "not enough."

This thought slowly seeps into daily life, quietly shaping choices:

"I can't afford this."
"If I give, there will be less left for me."

Thus, the mind tunes itself to fear rather than trust.

Yet abundance does not depend on circumstances — it lives in perception: in noticing what is already here.

How to Recognize It

The feeling of lack shows up in the body: gentle tightness in the chest, restlessness in the stomach, shallow breathing, tension in the shoulders.

Thoughts become hurried and urgent:

"I'll fall behind."
"There's no time."
"There won't be enough for everyone."

Consciousness narrows, the mind rushes, and the present moment is lost.

The first step is recognition: **the feeling of scarcity is not a fact but a perspective.**

The Turning Point

Transformation begins when you start to practice **gratitude and generosity** deliberately.

Gratitude is not an abstract feeling but a form of attention — the conscious act of noticing what is already present.

When attention shifts from what is missing to what *is*, awareness expands, and life begins to flow again.

Abundance is not a destination but an **experience** — the natural fullness of the present moment.

Practices

1. Gratitude Practice

Each day, choose three things you feel grateful for — even the smallest ones: a kind word, the freshness of the air, a smile.

Silently say:

"I am grateful."
Feel how the heart opens.

2. Giving in Small Steps

Offer something — time, attention, kindness, even a smile.

Notice how it feels to give without expecting anything in return.

This act re-tunes the mind to the frequency of abundance.

3. Conscious Awareness of Plenty

When you sense lack, ask yourself:

"What is still present right now?"
Look for what you can appreciate in this very moment.
Life is always giving something to see, to receive.

Shift in Vision

Abundance is not a measure of quantity but a **way of seeing.**

Gratitude is the eye of the heart: when you look through it, every moment reveals life as a gift already given.

To look upon wholeness instead of lack is not denial — it is awakening: the recognition that *there is always enough in the now.*

Scarcity is not reality, but **forgotten gratitude.**

Integrative Formula

Trigger → Thought → Emotion → Body → Impulse → Response

When "Response" is replaced by **Presence** and **value-based action,** the pattern dissolves — and abundance once again becomes your natural state.

Discovering Your Own Patterns

The practice of **mindful awareness** and **soul presence** invites you to see that every person lives through unique inner patterns.

Fear, anger, shame, or avoidance are all different faces of the same ignorance — the moment we forget that *in the present, all is already well.*

Recognition is not about finding fault, but about bringing light.

When you notice which pattern keeps returning in you, that is not weakness — it is awakening.

Every pattern carries potential: once you see it, it no longer guides you blindly.

Mindful awareness is the first step; **soul presence** is the next — when you not only perceive but also embrace every part of yourself.

Encouragement:

Discover which patterns move you. Look upon them with curiosity, not judgment.

Every recognition is a step home — to the meeting place of the soul and the Divine within you.

The Thought as Event, Not Reality

It is not the *content* of a thought that matters, but the *fact* that it is a thought.

Thoughts come and go; **Consciousness remains.**

In theological language: the thought is not the *Word* — the *Word* is the living Presence born within consciousness.

Mini-Practice (1 minute):

Focus on the breath.

When a thought arises, name it in a single word ("planning," "memory," "criticism"), and return to the breath.

Even in one minute, you can sense the seed of freedom.

You can extend this to 5, 10, or 15 minutes in a comfortable, upright but relaxed posture — and with practice, bring it into daily life.

The Power of Awareness Over Patterns

Patterns do not weaken through battle, but through **light.**

Three pillars guide this process:

1. **Notice** — awareness of body sensations.
2. **Allow** — spaciousness instead of resistance.
3. **Choose direction** — value-based action or gentle redirection of attention toward what is happening *now.*

3-Minute SOUL-Space (S.O.U.L.)

- **S:** *Sensing the breath*
- **O:** *Observing sensations*
- **U:** *Unfolding awareness through scanning the body*
- **L:** *Letting connect with the present as it is*
- This short protocol can be practiced several times a day to "reconnect" with the Source.

The Christ Consciousness Perspective

Christ Consciousness does not judge — it sees.

When you see a fault in another, see also their pain.

When you see shadow within yourself, recognize the light that lives in you.

Awareness — the gaze of Jesus within — dissolves patterns by illuminating them:

"The darkness cannot overcome the Light."

Prayer:

- *Inhale:* "I stand in Your light."
- *Exhale:* "I rest in Your love."

Practical Integration – Embodied Awareness

Breath Awareness + Naming Emotion

1. 30–60 seconds grounding in body sensations (feet, seat).
2. 2–3 minutes observing natural breathing.
3. When emotion appears, name it gently ("anxiety," "anger," "shame").
4. Breathe kindness with each inhale and exhale:

"Let it be as it is."

Micro-awareness prompt:
Ask several times a day:

"What is happening in me right now?"
   Start with small or even pleasant sensations before moving to difficult ones.

Reflect:

- What do I sense in the body?
- What kind of thought is running? (assumption / criticism / comparison)

"The Light of Envy" – Blessing Meditation (5 min)
Bring to heart someone who is successful.
Acknowledge the feeling: *"This envy is allowed."*
Recognize how much effort and suffering may lie behind their success.
Say silently:

"May you be blessed."
   Then add:
   "And may the same blessing unfold within me."

"The Wound Beneath Anger" – Healing Reflection

Recall a situation that triggered anger.

Notice the bodily signs.

Ask:

> *"What goodness am I protecting here?"*
> *(dignity, truth, boundary)*

Behavioral Re-Alignment – "One Step Now"

Choose a **2-minute action** — sending an email, washing a dish, taking a short walk.

Let the action align with your values (care, order, connection).

End with gratitude:

> *"Thank you."*

Closing Reflection – The Nature of Light

> *"When you see the mind, you are no longer the mind."*

The Soul recognizes itself.

Peace is not born from the absence of patterns,

but from the **fullness of Presence** that embraces them all.

V

About The World

28

The Body and the World as Sacredness

Seeing the Face of God in Forms
The world does not separate us from God — it leads us back to Him. Every form, every sound, every sensation of the body can become a doorway if we behold it with an open heart. The essence of contemplative practice is not to withdraw from the world, but to see it anew. For form, when seen through presence, is not a distraction but a transparent icon. Things do not exist by themselves — they exist in the light of God.

The vision with which we behold form is not ordinary sight; it is the vision of the heart — the consciousness that looks with love. When we see beyond form, we realize that what we perceive is not a mere object but a divine thought, a manifested intention. Form is not accidental or insignificant — it is a message rising from the fullness of Being.

Practice – Contemplating Form

Choose an object — a leaf, a candle, a chalice, or a stone. Place it before you. Observe it attentively, without naming or judging it. Notice its colors, its texture, the space around it. Beyond all perception, attune yourself to the presence through which the form exists. If your attention wanders, gently return. In time, you will recognize: behind the form is the same Presence that lives within you. Two gazes meet — yours, and the divine.

The Movement of the Body in God's Presence – Contemplative Walking

Movement is not the opposite of stillness or wisdom. Movement itself can be presence — if it is mindful. Contemplative walking is not a technique but a sacred attentiveness to every step. As the foot lifts, moves, and touches the earth, so the heart walks too — with awareness and humility. God is not only in inner silence but in every movement.

Practice – Contemplative Walking

Walk slowly along a chosen path. Notice how your body moves — how the foot rolls forward, how you feel the ground. Do not hurry. Follow your breath. If thoughts arise, notice them and return to the sensation of walking. Silently say: *"I am here."* Every step is sacred.

Hearing the World with the Ear of God

Sounds do not separate; they return us. Every sound is a vibration of Being. When we do not label or interpret, we begin to hear the silence behind it. Sound and silence together are God's speech.

Practice – Listening Meditation

Sit quietly. Allow the sounds of your surroundings to reach you — birds, wind, cars, human voices. Do not seek them — let them come. Listen with an open heart. Notice what happens in the silence between sounds. God often speaks not *in* the sound, but *through* the space behind it.

Eating as Eucharistic Presence

Eating is not a profane act. When we are present, every bite becomes an expression of gratitude. Every taste, scent, and motion speaks of the miracle of life. Bread is not just bread — it is life. Water is not merely drink — it is presence. The body receives the world of God, and when we are attentive, the soul responds with thanksgiving.

Practice – Mindful Eating

Take a small piece of food. Before eating, reflect briefly on how many hands, fields, rains, and rays of sunlight made this moment possible. Look closely, smell it, feel its weight. Then slowly take a bite and notice the taste, the texture, the movement in your mouth. Do not rush. Be present. Every bite is a gift of life. Breathe, and silently give thanks after each one.

Breath as the Rhythm of God

Breathing is the most direct path to God. Nothing must be done — only allowed. Every inhalation is the flow of the Spirit. Every exhalation is surrender. The first and last act of our life is breath — and between them, it is with us always. The Spirit lives in every breath.

Through the breath, not only does the body rest, but consciousness is purified. It is as if God continually passes through us. Breathing is not merely a biological function, but a prayer — an inner rhythm that forever returns to the divine presence.

Practice – Awareness of Breath

Sit upright. Bring your attention to your breathing: where do you feel it most — the nose, the chest, the belly? Do not change it — simply observe. If the mind wanders, return gently. This is attention to God. And God responds — with Presence. With every breath, you affirm once more:

"I am here. And You are here."

29

The Illusion of the Modern World – When Being Was Replaced by Production

Since the Industrial Revolution, Western civilization has gradually embraced a value system that measures human worth almost entirely by productivity and performance. Work has become the religion of the modern age, and economic growth its collective god — an altar upon which most people make daily offerings.

At every level of society — in education, workplaces, and even within families — we are taught that we are valuable only when we are doing, producing, or improving. The art of *being* has been replaced by the compulsion to *do*, and silence or stillness has become suspicious, as if non-action were a sign of laziness or uselessness.

This conditioning runs deep within the collective mind. Most of us learned as children that love and approval are conditional — earned only through achievement. Parents, often unconsciously, pass this belief on to their children, and generation by generation, self-worth becomes dependent on external validation rather than inner peace or authenticity.

The world accelerates, technology advances, yet humanity drifts further from itself. In the endless pursuit of success, status, and accomplishment, many feel empty and exhausted — no longer remembering what they are striving for.

The Illusion of Compulsory Activity

The modern world whispers: *work, produce, prove yourself — only then will you deserve your place.* This belief is no longer an economic rule but a moral law. Those who pause, rest, or contemplate are quickly labeled "unproductive." Thus we have built a collective illusion in which productivity has replaced being as the measure of worth.

From childhood we learn that doing nothing equals being nothing — a message that follows us into adulthood. Yet constant activity gives only the illusion of meaning. The restless busyness of modern life is often a flight from silence, where we might have to face ourselves. The mind fears stillness because in stillness it might discover it has nothing to prove.

But in a culture addicted to performance, such a realization feels dangerous. So we keep running — and quietly burn out.

Human beings, however, are not machines. Our essence is not production, but conscious, loving presence. When the sanctity of being is sacrificed on the altar of productivity, life becomes a function rather than a miracle. From this distortion arise envy, anxiety, and depression — the soul's cry for its natural rhythm. Life then ceases to be *lived* and becomes a *task*. And the harder we try to meet expectations, the farther we drift from peace.

The Effect of Social Conditioning

The culture of performance distorts not only individuals but entire societies. Media, advertising, and social networks continually portray "a meaningful life" as one of success, activity, and progress. Rest, stillness, and non-doing rarely appear in a positive light.

This message suppresses the natural rhythm of life — the sacred alternation of activity and rest, expression and receptivity. Humanity thus falls into a double trap: external demands and internal pressure. The body and soul both grow weary beneath the tyranny of "more, faster, better."

Stress, distraction, insomnia, and burnout are not personal failures — they are symptoms of our civilization. The soul hungers for silence, but the noise of the world rarely pauses long enough for us to listen.

The Madness of the World

Modern humanity believes itself sane, yet its mind is dreaming. It fears silence because silence does not produce; it condemns slowness because it yields no profit; it calls introspection selfish because it threatens the noise. Thus we have built the *temple of noise*, where the whole world now worships.

> **"A time will come when people will go mad, and if they see someone who is not mad, they will say: 'You are insane, for you are not like us.'"**

— Saint Anthony, Sayings of the Desert Fathers

That time has come. The one who lives quietly is suspect. The one who does not hurry is "left behind." The one who does not consume is "failing." And the one who finds God within is called strange. But it is not silence that is madness — it is the noise we have named normal.

The warning of the Desert Fathers now resounds anew: the world is asleep and takes its dream for reality. The awakening always begins when someone dares to say no to the collective dream — and chooses to remain in silence.

The Recognition of Inner Freedom

Those who accept the narrative that their worth is defined by achievement eventually become enslaved by it. Anxiety, competition, and the urge to prove oneself are the modern forms of bondage. People are afraid to stop, fearing that doing nothing will make them disappear.

But this fear is only a thought. The value of life does not lie in what we *do*, but in how deeply we are *present* within it. This realization is not intellectual but experiential. The moment one allows oneself to do nothing — simply to breathe and *be* — a quiet peace begins to arise.

This peace does not come from idleness but from conscious presence. In that stillness, comparison and striving dissolve, and something eternal shines through — life itself.

The system around us is not evil, only unconscious. And it is unconscious-ness that makes the world restless, noisy, and exhausted. Yet each of us can awaken from this dream. The first step toward awakening is to realize: we have a choice. We do not need to follow the world's rhythm when it no longer serves the peace of the soul.

The Awakening of Consciousness and the New Rhythm

True freedom begins when we awaken to the fact that we are not our minds, nor the roles imposed upon us by society. The awareness that observes all of this is inherently free and whole. When this is realized, the compulsion to perform begins to fade.

We can allow ourselves to pause, to breathe, to rediscover the joy of simple existence. Presence is not passivity — it is the highest form of action: the natural flow of life guided not by ego, but by consciousness itself.

When we learn once more simply *to be*, our actions become purer, more authentic, and more loving. No longer driven by external expectations, but guided by inner peace. We cease to move at the rhythm of society and begin to move with the rhythm of the Spirit — the quiet pulse through which all life beats.

Life itself is sacred — existence is sacred. Every moment in which we turn from lack toward wholeness reconnects us with this truth. Anything that nourishes rather than drains — a heartfelt conversation, an act of creation, a quiet walk, or attentive presence with another — is already sacred, for it serves life.

Love and compassion, the simple act of caring, are sacred because they sustain both community and soul.

As the Stoics taught, human nature is communal — we are made *for one another.* No one thrives in isolation. Helping others is helping ourselves, for every act that moves toward unity returns to us.

> *"All that happens is interconnected; you are part of the whole. What benefits the community benefits you as well."*
> — Marcus Aurelius, Meditations *IV.40*

Contemplative Question

"If you are not defined by your work or your actions, then who are you?"

This question does not ask for a logical answer, but for silence.

Its response is not a thought but an experience — found in that still inner space where we allow ourselves simply to exist, and recognize that being itself is already wholeness.

30

Sacred Work – When Action Becomes Prayer

Human life is not composed of contemplation alone but also of action.

Yet the modern world often separates the two, as if work and awareness were opposites.

In the great spiritual traditions, however, contemplation and work form a single whole.

The ancient monastic principle *ora et labora* — "pray and work" — reminds us that every action can become prayer when done with presence and attention.

Work itself is neither sacred nor profane; it becomes what our consciousness makes of it.

When driven by urgency, fear, or the need to prove oneself, work separates us from the Source of Being.

But when accompanied by awareness and gratitude, even the simplest task becomes transfigured.

Then work ceases to be mere survival — it becomes a practice of consciousness, a path through which the soul learns to be fully present in every moment.

Contemplation in Action

The contemplative person does not flee the world but becomes fully present within it.

The attention cultivated in meditation is tested in daily life — in washing dishes, writing, teaching, gardening, or speaking with another.

Each act can be sacred when the focus is not on outcome, but on presence.

Thus, contemplation is not passivity, but the art of presence within action.

Sacred work is not about doing extraordinary things but about doing ordinary things with extraordinary awareness.

Whoever works with full attention is already praying, even without words.

Whoever works with love manifests the presence of God in the world.

The Balance of Silence and Activity

Modern people often lose themselves in action, forgetting the inner silence that nourishes life.

True wholeness, however, lies in balance.

Contemplation feeds action, and action leads us back to contemplation — like inhalation and exhalation sustaining the rhythm of the soul.

As Saint Benedict taught, work is not a burden but a service — the way through which God manifests in human hands.

When we see this, every activity can become meditation.

The question is not *what* we do, but *how* we do it.

Work as a Path of Self-Knowledge

Work is one of the deepest mirrors for self-discovery.

While working, patterns of impatience, control, ego, and fear arise — not as faults, but as opportunities for awareness.

When we observe ourselves in action, we begin to notice the silent witness behind the doer — the consciousness that simply watches.

Contemplative work is not an escape from the world, but its sanctification.

When presence infuses every act, work becomes prayer and the day becomes liturgy.

The sacred and the ordinary are no longer divided — every moment becomes cooperation with God.

Practical Steps Toward Sacred Work

Begin the day with awareness. Before doing anything, pause for a few moments and remember: every act today can be prayer through awareness. Feel your body resting in bed, sense the morning stillness. As you drink your coffee, notice its warmth, aroma, and taste — the light, the sounds of morning.

Stay connected to the body while working. Feel each movement, the rhythm of breath, the motion of your hands. Let attention bring you back to the present moment.

Work with gratitude. Remember that work is a gift — a chance for consciousness to express the creative force and to serve others. The street sweeper keeps the world clean; the office worker maintains order; the craftsman sustains what others depend on.

Take conscious pauses. Just as the day has dawn and dusk, so the mind needs intervals of rest.

Release attachment to results. Do what is yours to do — then let God bear the fruit.

31

Digital Noise and the Loss of Attention – When Technology Rules the Mind

In recent decades, technological progress has transformed human life on an unprecedented scale.

Digital devices, the internet, social media, and constant connectivity have ushered in a new era — the age of attention.

Modern society has turned not only our time but also our attention into a commodity.

Every screen, feed, and notification competes to hold the mind captive for as long as possible.

But the price is high: the gradual loss of silence, presence, and inner peace.

Technology was created to serve humanity — to make life easier.

Yet today, it is often humanity that serves technology.

Most people instinctively reach for their phones whenever a moment of emptiness appears.

Attention is fractured into countless pieces, and the mind can no longer find stillness.

The digital world generates constant noise — not only around us, but within us.

Attention as the Gateway of Consciousness

Attention is one of the greatest treasures of human consciousness.

Where attention goes, life flows.

But when it is constantly diverted, we lose connection with ourselves.

Social media, advertising, and the rapid flow of information train the mind to be restless, fragmented, and shallow.

Concentration and deep presence have become rare skills.

The digital environment leaves no room for boredom — yet boredom is the doorway to the inner life.

In the past, when one paused, thought could deepen, and consciousness could turn inward.

Today, when we pause, we instantly reach for stimulation — and lose the connection to the inner silence where the Spirit speaks.

Attention, therefore, is not merely a mental function but a spiritual gate: wherever we direct it, that becomes the quality of our life.

Noise and the Absence of Inner Silence

Digital noise overstimulates not only the mind but also the heart.

Constant notifications, visual stimuli, and an endless flow of information keep the nervous system in a perpetual state of alert.

This is a form of subtle stress: the body cannot rest, and the soul cannot sink into depth.

Modern humans are, paradoxically, always connected — yet increasingly lonely.

To restore balance, we must consciously seek genuine human contact.

Go for a walk, have coffee with someone, join a local event, play games, do sports, or simply talk — to rediscover the warmth of presence beyond the screen.

Even a brief, kind exchange can remind us that others, too, hunger for connection.

Digital noise not only steals attention but also distorts reality.

Social media has become the breeding ground for comparison and envy, where people measure themselves against the idealized lives of others.

This constant comparison breeds insecurity, anxiety, and dissatisfaction.

Attention drifts from the present moment into the realms of lack and longing.

Calling the Mind Back to Presence

The first step toward awakening from technological noise is recognizing how deeply it has captured our attention.

We do not need to reject technology — only to become aware of when we are using it, and when it is using us.

By setting down the phone, turning off notifications, and directing our awareness to the breath, the sounds of nature, or the sensations of the body, we begin to return home to the present moment.

Presence is not an escape from the world but a return to what is real.

The Spirit does not speak through the glare of screens but through the quiet stillness of the heart.

As the mind is reclaimed from distraction, consciousness expands, and the Presence of God becomes tangible within.

In this space, technology no longer dominates — it serves.

Practical mindfulness means reducing or eliminating unconscious scrolling and unnecessary applications.

Create daily *windows of silence*, times when your phone rests in *Do Not Disturb* mode, allowing only essential calls to pass through.

Turn off every non-essential notification.

Each intentional act of simplification restores attention and reopens the inner ear to the voice of the Soul.

Attention as a Sacred Power

Attention does not wander randomly; it follows what the heart deems important.

Thus, a conscious life is nothing less than the sanctification of attention.

Reclaiming our attention from digital noise is not restriction — it is liberation.

Attention not only observes reality but shapes it: what it sees, it brings to life.

When we place our attention upon the Spirit, the Spirit becomes our reality.

VI

Completion and Return to the Source

32

The Christ Within – Pure Awareness

In every human heart there dwells a quiet and unchanging Presence. The contemplative Christian tradition knows this as *the Christ within* — the divine spark of pure awareness.

This pure awareness is the very essence of our true being, and recognizing its qualities brings us closer to the living Presence of God within.

It reveals itself in five ways:

Accepting:

Pure awareness turns toward all things with unconditional acceptance.

In this inner Presence, nothing is rejected — Christ within us loves and embraces everything just as it is, as Jesus loved without condition.

All-embracing:

Pure awareness includes and holds everything.

Nothing exists outside of it.

It reminds us that Christ is "all and in all."

It is what we have always been — the luminous field of divine Presence that unites all life.

Non-judging:

The Christ consciousness within does not judge.

It is the awareness reflected in Jesus' words: *"Do not judge, and you will not be judged."*

This divine Presence beholds creation with compassion, not dividing it into good or evil, but seeing all in the light of divine love.

Omnipresent:

Pure awareness is boundless and infinite, like God Himself.

There is no place or moment where the consciousness of Christ is absent.

God is not confined by space or time — His Presence fills the world and our souls alike.

Universal:

This awareness is the same Presence in every human being.

The Christ who lives in you also lives in everyone.

It is the one divine life pulsing through all existence — as Paul wrote, *"It is no longer I who live, but Christ who lives in me."*

The same Christ dwells in every heart, without distinction.

To recognize these qualities is to realize that our true nature is rooted in God.

Pure awareness — the Christ within — is accepting, all-embracing, non-judging, ever-present, and equally alive in all.

When we awaken to this truth, we discover that within our own soul shines the Kingdom of God — the realm of love and unity.

The Path of Attention and Silence

The purpose of contemplative Christian practice is to awaken to this inner divine Presence.

Through attention, stillness, and silence we draw near to the Christ within.

When we intentionally rest our awareness in the present moment — without judgment, without distraction — we become receptive to the voice of God in the heart.

Silence is not emptiness; it is living Presence.

It is there that we hear the "still, small voice" through which God speaks.

In contemplative prayer or meditation, we simply rest before God — who appears within us.

As one teaching says, silent prayer is "the prayer of the heart," being with God who is already within, through the Holy Spirit.

By surrendering to this Presence, we recognize that we are already one with Him.

Attention — whether to the breath, a sacred word (like the Jesus Prayer), or the felt immediacy of being — gradually leads us into the inner sanctuary where Christ dwells.

Beyond words and thoughts, we enter the quiet depth of faith and Presence where God waits for us.

In that stillness, our soul unites with the consciousness of Christ — discovering Him not as an idea, but as a living reality within.

As Scripture declares: *"Christ in you, the hope of glory."*

When we share in the awareness of Jesus Himself, we realize that He truly is "the way, the truth, and the life" within us.

Through the path of attention and silence, we meet Christ in the depths of our own heart — where He has always lived, though we seldom noticed.

Liberation from the Prison of Illusion

As we recognize the Christ within — pure awareness itself — we begin to awaken from the prison of illusion.

What illusions?

The illusion of separation, of isolation, of being cut off from God and from one another.

The ego, our small self-image, makes us believe we are alone and must struggle to prove our worth, judging ourselves and others, striving as though life were apart from the divine.

These illusions — of separateness, judgment, fear, and lovelessness — are the roots of spiritual bondage.

But in the stillness of meditation, as we open to pure awareness, these illusions dissolve.

We see that we were never truly apart from God.

The idea that He is distant or that we must reach Him fades away.

As Jesus said: *"The kingdom of God is within you."*

God's reign, His presence and love, are not far away — they are here, within the soul.

When this truth dawns, every illusion of distance or delay falls away.

We realize that we are already citizens of heaven, if we let the consciousness of Christ live through us.

This awakening is like light filling a dark room: the darkness of illusion vanishes at once.

We cease believing the false stories about who we are and recognize ourselves as children of God, through whom Christ lives and acts.

To identify with Christ — to know our true Self as the divine Self — is to be freed from every chain.

Then Jesus' promise is fulfilled: *"You will know the truth, and the truth will set you free."*

Knowing Christ as the living Truth within, we step out of fear and guilt into the freedom of the soul.

In the Light of Jesus' Teaching

Throughout His life, Jesus pointed us to this inner reality.

He did not come to found an external religion but to restore the living communion between God and humanity — within us.

When He said, *"I am the way, the truth, and the life,"* He revealed Himself as the light of consciousness that illumines every human being.

He is the Way, because the path to Him is not external law but inner union.

He is the Truth, because His pure awareness is the only foundation on which life can rest.

And He is the Life, because His Presence is the life of all.

"In Him was life, and the life was the light of men."

When Jesus said, *"The kingdom of God is within you,"* He invited us to recognize God's reign in the sanctuary of the heart.

The seed of heaven already lies within.

It is not something that will arrive later or elsewhere — it is here, now, as the temple of the Holy Spirit within the soul.

God is not distant; He is nearer than our own breath.

When this truth awakens in us, prayer, sacrament, and faith itself become living encounters with the Christ who dwells within.

Thus the greatest commandment — to love — can only be fulfilled through

Christ consciousness.

If Christ is alive in everyone, then "love your neighbor as yourself" means seeing Christ in others as in ourselves.

We can no longer judge or exclude, for we have seen our shared divinity.

Jesus' prayer, *"That they may all be one, as You, Father, are in Me and I in You,"* is fulfilled when we realize that the same Christ lives in all, and we are one Body in Him.

The Eternal Presence Here and Now

We have reached the end of this book, yet stand at the threshold of a new beginning.

Along the contemplative path we have discovered that the goal we sought — enlightenment, salvation, union with God — was never far away.

It has always been within us.

The aim of practice is not a distant reward but the grace revealed in this very moment.

God does not delay His Presence; it surrounds and fills us even now.

What we have longed for has always lived in our hearts.

Let this closing thought be a gentle reminder: the Kingdom of God is within you.

The spark of eternal life that Christ carries burns already in your soul.

There is nowhere to run, nothing to force — only to allow the Presence to unfold within.

With every breath, remember: *Emmanuel — God with us, God within us.*

The Christ within is the Eternal Now, the "I Am" in whose nearness the soul finds rest.

Even in this moment, as you read these words, He is here.

In your silence, in the sheer fact of your being, the subtle music of Christ consciousness is already resonating.

If you listen, you will hear it more clearly.

If you open your heart, you will feel it more deeply.

And if you remain in this Presence, you will know the peace and unity to which Jesus called us — the homecoming of the soul to its true dwelling in

God.

So let us end with this realization: the Christ we sought has lived within us from the beginning.

The light of pure awareness has never left; only we needed to learn to see it.

Now, in every moment, we can remember this truth.

The Eternal Presence carries us, and we may live consciously and lovingly within it.

This realization is our freedom and salvation.

Let gratitude and sacred silence fill the soul for this unspeakable gift.

God is with us — God lives within us — now and forever. Amen.

33

Epilogue – The Key Is Recognition

As we have journeyed through the path of contemplation in these pages, a reality has gradually unfolded before us — one that does not need to be attained, only recognized: that the very Consciousness in which all things appear — the body, emotions, thoughts, the world, and every form — is none other than the living Presence of Christ within us.

This consciousness is not an abstract concept, nor a special state. It is the open, spacious, aware presence that has always been with us. When we were born, it was in this awareness that we took our first breath; and when we rest in silence, we return once more to our true home. This presence is what the saints called God, the mystics recognized as Christ, and the awakened soul knows as the Self.

Jesus did not merely speak of the Kingdom of God — He revealed it within: *"The Kingdom of God is within you."* This is not a promise but a living truth. When we begin to recognize that the awareness which perceives is itself God, a profound transformation begins. We no longer seek God outside, nor confine Him to concepts, but allow Him to reveal Himself from within.

This knowing is not intellectual but experiential. Nothing needs to be added — only to be still and return, again and again, to contemplative presence.

There, where there is no judgment, only awareness.

There, where there is no separation, only unity.

There, where Spirit touches Spirit.

And finally, there, where we can say: *"It is no longer I who live, but Christ who lives in me."* Not as a belief, but as the deepest reality — the truth that has always been.

May this recognition be a blessing to you. And once it is known, do not cling to it — but live from it.

May the peace of Presence guide your path. Christ lives within you.

Written in Spain, on the land of the mystics — Málaga.

— Atilion

Practices in Depth

Body Scan – The Root of Presence

Sit or lie down comfortably. Allow your body to find its own natural position.

There is no special posture required — only one that feels safe and at ease.

If you wish, gently close your eyes.

Take your attention to your breath... and be aware of the in breath and the out breath st your belly as it rises and falling back.

You don't need to quiet your mind — simply allow yourself to *be here, now.*

Your body is already present — you are only inviting your awareness home to it.

Now bring your attention slowly to your left foot's toes.

You don't need to feel anything special — just notice that they exist.

Maybe there is warmth, tingling, or perhaps nothing at all.

Whatever is there, it is perfectly fine.

Now anchor your attention to the breath and as you breath in go down to your toes and its feelings like if you breath in to your toes and as you breath out go upwards till to your nostril as you exhale and now again breath in to your toes and do this for 1-3 minutes or as you like, when you decided to leave you breathe out and be there for a bit see how the feelings of the toes dissolves and you just aware the awareness and your nostrils. Now go back to your left feet.

Slowly let your awareness travel upward — to the soles of your feet, the heels, the ankles. Feel in depth the feelings here

If you sense tension somewhere, don't try to change it.

Just allow it to be — like a guest you no longer need to chase away.

Move to your calves. Feel the gentle weight of the muscles beneath the skin,

the subtle flow of blood, the living presence of your legs.

The body is not an obstacle — it is the living stream of life carrying you.

Now feel your knees, your thighs.

You may sense discomfort or ease — whatever is there,

And with that, the light of awareness is already shining on your experience.

Breathe into your pelvis. Let the breath fill this space.

This is your center of life — the place of stability and grounding.

If you notice your thoughts drifting away,

smile gently within: *"I wandered off — and I noticed."*

That noticing is the very moment of awakening. Now repeat this procedure with your right feet. After that

Move upward to the abdomen and the chest.

Feel the movement of breath —

the belly rising and falling, the chest expanding and releasing.

Nothing to control. The breath happens by itself.

You are only the witness — the consciousness through which everything breathes.

Now bring awareness to your shoulders, arms, and hands in depth. You may feel tinglings in the fingertips thats okay too they are very sensitive.

Feel how they rest, how they hold or release.

In your palms lives the present moment — always open, always receiving.

Finally, let your awareness move to your neck, your face. First the mouth, the lips then the nostrils and after that slowly your eyes and its area after that your forehead.

If you feel lightness, that's fine. If heaviness, that too.

Every feeling is welcome in this field of awareness.

Now slowly go back from head to feet any embody the whole body. Let your awareness hold your full body.

Now that you have moved through your whole body,

sense how your attention has become a single gentle field of light enveloping your entire being.

This is you — consciousness itself, holding everything without possessing it.

Stay here for a 5-10 minutes.

And when you open your eyes again,

know that this awareness has not disappeared.

You are simply continuing your meditation —

now with open eyes, as you move through the world.

Breath Awareness – Resting the Mind in the Breath

Sit comfortably with an upright but relaxed spine.

Let your feet rest on the ground, your hips slightly higher than your knees.

You may use a meditation cushion if you like.

Allow your body to support itself — there is nothing to fix.

Take a deep breath in through the nose...

and slowly, softly exhale through the mouth.

Notice how the air enters and leaves — each breath happening on its own.

Do not try to breathe *correctly*.

No need to slow down or control it.

Breathing happens — you simply notice.

Feel the cool air touching your nostrils,

and how it leaves, slightly warmer.

Perhaps you sense the movement of your chest,

or the rise and fall of your belly.

Choose where the breath feels most alive — and stay there, gently.

Thoughts will appear. That's perfectly fine.

The mind's nature is to create thoughts.

You don't need to fight them.

As soon as you notice you've drifted away,

say quietly to yourself: *"Thinking,"*

and gently return to the breath —

as if coming home.

You'll notice that each return brings a deeper sense of ease.

Not because you are doing it "better,"

but because attention is learning to rest in itself.

If you feel tension, try breathing *into* it —
not pushing it away, but embracing it.
The breath is like a friend who softly holds everything
you once tried to avoid.
Now notice how breathing doesn't only happen *in* you.
The air comes from the world, flows into you, and returns again.
You and the world move in the same breath.
There is no boundary — Spirit and world breathe together.
If the breath deepens, stay with it.
If it remains shallow, that's also fine.
Don't try to change anything.
This practice isn't about perfection —
it's about allowing each moment to be as it is.
Sit like this for a while.
With each inhale, feel: *"I am alive."*
With each exhale: *"I let it be."*
The breath is your teacher,
calling you home to the present in every moment.
When you rise, do not leave it behind.
Let it accompany you as you walk, speak, or listen.
Now it is no longer that *you* are watching the breath —
but rather, awareness itself is breathing:
life moving through life.

Open Awareness
Sit comfortably and allow your body to rest.
There is nothing to do. Awareness itself can now rest in awareness.
Begin by noticing: *you are aware.*
Not of anything in particular — simply of awareness itself.
There is nothing to reach for.
Just allow perception to remain open.
Perhaps there is silence.
Notice what that silence feels like — not heard by the ears, but sensed by

awareness.

Perhaps a thought arises. Don't stop it. Just notice: *"Thought."*
And let it dissolve back into the open field.
Maybe there is a feeling — pleasant or heavy.
Awareness notices that too.
See how experiences appear and disappear,
yet something always remains that knows them.
That unchanging presence — that is *you*.
Pure consciousness, in which everything is born and fades away.
You don't need to cling even to silence,
for silence too is an experience that changes.
Awareness itself does not change.
It is that which witnesses every change.
Rest here.
There is nothing to achieve,
for what you seek is already here — it is *you*.
Awareness is like space:
it does not exclude anything, nor is it trapped by anything.
Whenever you notice that you are aware — you are home.
When a thought comes — that's awareness too.
When there is silence — that too is awareness.
Stay with this recognition for a few moments.
Rest in the one who has always been here.
And when you open your eyes,
know that you have not left meditation —
you have simply let the world enter
the same awareness in which all things arise.

Observing Thoughts – The Waves of the Mind

Sit comfortably and close your eyes.
Let your body rest like a lake whose surface is slowly calming.
Take a deep breath, and let your attention turn inward.
For a few minutes, you may follow the breath,
or, if you know the open-awareness practice,

observe how thoughts arise within that same vast space.

Do not try to stop the mind.

You don't need to silence thoughts —

just watch them, as you would watch waves on the lake.

You are not making the waves — you simply see them.

Observe as a thought appears:

a picture, a sentence, a memory, a plan.

Just notice: *"Thought."*

And let it drift away.

No need to chase it, no need to push it down.

If you find yourself caught in a story —

"What I should have done differently," or "What will happen tomorrow"

—

simply notice that you noticed.

That moment of recognition is awakening itself.

Now try to sense where thoughts come from.

A moment before they appear, there is nothing — only vastness.

Then a form arises, and fades again.

Awareness is like the sky,

and thoughts are clouds moving through it.

You don't need to clear the sky —

the sky does not resent the clouds.

If a thought returns strongly,

observe it too,

then gently return to the breath or the body — your safe home.

Notice that thoughts are impermanent.

One comes, another goes —

and you remain, the one who sees.

You are not the thought — you are the one who is aware of it.

Now let your attention widen.

Don't focus on any single thought, but sense the entire space in which they appear.

This space does not become confused; it does not judge —

it simply allows everything to come and go.
If there is silence, that's fine.
If there are many thoughts, that too is fine.
Meditation is not about the *state* you are in,
but about whether you can *see* what is.
Stay here for a few breaths.
Inhale and feel: *"I am here."*
Exhale and feel: *"I let it be."*
As you slowly open your eyes,
try to see the world this way too:
people, situations, thoughts —
all arising in the same consciousness
and returning to the same stillness.
You are not the wave —
you are the ocean that lovingly holds every wave.

Observing Emotions – The Expansion of the Heart (The Dialogue of Awareness and Feeling)

Sit comfortably and allow your body to rest.
Take a few deep, natural breaths.
Don't control them — let them come and go on their own.
Notice the air entering... and leaving.
The breath is not *you* — you are aware of it.
This awareness is the doorway to Presence.
Now, for a moment, don't focus on the breath — focus on awareness itself.
Notice that you are aware.
Not of anything specific — simply of being here.
This is pure presence. Nothing to reach for, only to recognize.
Rest here for a while...
If there is silence, notice the silence.
If a thought appears, it appears *in* awareness.
If a feeling arises — it too is part of awareness's play.
Now gently bring attention into the body and ask inwardly:

"Where do I feel something right now?"
It might be in the chest, the belly, the throat,
the shoulders, or somewhere else.
Emotions often speak through the body —
the body is the language of the soul.
Simply notice where life is most vivid.
No need to analyze or name it.
It could be warmth, tightness, numbness, emptiness, vibration, or stillness.
Whatever it is — allow it to be seen.
As the feeling shows itself, don't call it good or bad.
Simply say within: *"I feel."*
And stay with it for a few breaths.
Don't push it away — let it rest in the light of awareness.
Now allow your attention to expand again.
Don't focus on the feeling, but on the space in which the feeling appears.
Like looking at the sky: the cloud is visible, but the sky remains unmoved.
Awareness is open once more.
Rest in this openness for a breath or two...
then gently bring attention back to the body.
Ask again: *"What do I feel now?"*
Perhaps the sensation has moved — from the chest to the throat, or to the stomach.
Just notice, and breathe through it.
You may use your breath as in the body scan meditation, breathing in and out from the fields where are the feelings.
This practice is not about control,
but about the natural rhythm between awareness and feeling —
like the ebb and flow of the tide: awareness expands, then returns to the body.
If pain, fear, or anger arises — breathe through it.
Do not try to fix it.
Awareness does not *heal something* —

it recognizes that everything is already born within its own light.

Allow this movement to happen naturally:

sometimes attention rests in a bodily sensation,

sometimes in vast awareness.

Nothing to do — only to allow life to reveal itself.

Soon you will notice: feelings are not obstacles but doorways.

Every place in the body where you feel something

is an entrance into consciousness.

Every emotion, when allowed, dissolves back into the vastness of awareness

and becomes peace.

Stay here for a few more breaths, in warm, open attention.

Breathe in and feel: *"I am here."*

Breathe out and feel: *"I let it be."*

And when you open your eyes again,

know that this movement — awareness, feeling, awareness —

continues in every moment.

The world you see is not different

from what now appeared within you.

This is the expansion of the heart —

when awareness no longer flees from feeling,

but recognizes that feeling too is itself.

Further Teachings and Courses

If you wish to explore more deeply and experience the theurgic meditations described in this book, visit www.newteurgia.com where you'll find my personal and online teachings, theurgic meditation evenings, and the live online *Conscious Presence* course.

Loved the book? Take the next step — **bring the teachings to life** through guided practice, live discussions, and the shared radiance of awakened souls.

Join our sacred Practice Group on Facebook — where seekers of Light gather to deepen their Hermetic and Christ-conscious practice.

Step beyond reading — *experience the transformation.*

Meet fellow practitioners online.

Group name: New Teurgia - Practice Group for Christ Consciousness and Spirituality

If you can't find it, look for the current link on www.newteurgia.com

Recommended Readings

The Journey Does Not End with These Pages

Understanding is a living process — an ever-deepening unfolding within the one who sincerely seeks.

The words of the masters below can help you recognize the light of consciousness in everyday life, right where you are.

Jon Kabat-Zinn

1. Wherever You Go, There You Are – Mindfulness Meditation in Everyday Life

A gentle and practical guide to returning, again and again, to the present moment — the natural home of awareness.

2. Coming to Our Senses – Healing Ourselves and the World Through Mindfulness

Mindfulness is not merely a technique, but the original way of being human — the path of the awakened heart.

Yongey Mingyur Rinpoche

1. The Joy of Living – Unlocking the Secret and Science of Happiness

Reveals how happiness is not something to be achieved, but the natural state of the mind, recognized in stillness.

2. Joyful Wisdom – Embracing Change and Finding Freedom

A deeply personal teaching on how suffering transforms into freedom when seen through the light of awareness.

3. In Love with the World – A Monk's Journey Through the Bardos of Living and Dying

The master's intimate account of his near-death experience and direct realization of the boundless nature of consciousness.

Pope Francis
1. Let Us Dream – The Path to a Better Future
Written during the pandemic, yet timeless in its message: every crisis is a call of the Spirit, inviting us to rediscover trust, community, and love.
2. A Good Life – 15 Essential Habits for Living with Hope and Joy
Simple yet profound spiritual habits that turn ordinary life into prayer and thanksgiving.

Adyashanti
Resurrecting Jesus – Embodying the Spirit of a Revolutionary Mystic
A luminous exploration of Jesus' life and teachings as the archetype of inner awakening.

The crucifixion and resurrection are revealed as symbols of consciousness transformed — a journey that unfolds within every human heart.

Closing Reflection
These works speak in the diverse languages of different ages and traditions, yet all point to the same Reality —
to the living Christ who longs to awaken in every heart.
In silence, in presence, and in surrender,
the same Light shines —
the Spirit who has dwelt within you from the very beginning.

Sources and Inspirations

The insights, reflections, and contemplative practices presented in this book arise from the author's own inner experience — the fruit of years of meditation, prayer, and contemplative living.

The cited scriptures, mystics, and spiritual sources that have inspired and illuminated this path include:

Sacred Scripture and Christian Sources

The Holy Bible – quotations primarily from the Gospels of John and Luke:

"I in them, and You in Me..." (John 17:23)
"Father, forgive them, for they know not what they do." (Luke 23:34)
"Blessed are the pure in heart, for they shall see God." (Matthew 5:8)

Saint Teresa of Ávila – *The Interior Castle (El Castillo Interior o Las Moradas, 1577)*

Meister Eckhart – Sermons and Meditations

Saint John of the Cross – *The Dark Night of the Soul (La noche oscura del alma, c. 1578–1586)*

Johannes Tauler – *Sermons*

Heinrich Suso – *The Little Book of Truth (Büchlein der Wahrheit)*

Angelus Silesius – *The Cherubinic Wanderer (Cherubinischer Wandersmann, 1657)*

Saint Anthony the Great – *The Sayings of the Desert Fathers (Apophthegmata Patrum)*

Saint Gregory of Nyssa – *The Life of Moses (De Vita Moysis)*

Origen – *Homilies on the Song of Songs (Homiliae in Canticum Canticorum)*

The Nag Hammadi Library in English, ed. James M. Robinson (HarperOne, 1988)

Jingjiao (Nestorian Christianity) – *The Xi'an Stele* (*Jingjiao-bei*, A.D. 781)

Hermetic and Eastern Traditions

Hermes Trismegistus – *Corpus Hermeticum*
(on the divine nature of consciousness and the recognition of Unity)
Laozi – *Tao Te Ching*
(on natural presence and the wisdom of non-action)
Buddha – *Dhammapada*
(on mindfulness, compassion, and liberation)
Marcus Aurelius and **Epictetus** – *Meditations* and Stoic Fragments
(on the unity of the cosmos and the harmony of reason and virtue)

Modern Inspirations

Jon Kabat-Zinn – *Full Catastrophe Living*
(the Western approach to mindfulness and present-moment awareness)
Yongey Mingyur Rinpoche – *The Joy of Living*
(the recognition of the mind's nature and the inner science of meditation)
Thich Nhat Hanh – *The Miracle of Mindfulness*
(the practice of awareness in daily life and compassionate presence)

Author's and Legal Notice

Its teachings are not intended as dogmatic instruction, but as an invitation to inner realization and the direct experience of union with God.

All quotations and references are included with the intention of respectful acknowledgment of their sources.

This work is published under the pen name "Atilion" for public reference. The real identity of the author is disclosed here solely for legal protection and copyright purposes.

For legal purposes, the real identity of the author is Attila Sándor Puskás.

All moral rights and copyright are asserted under both names.

The author and publisher disclaim any responsibility for any direct or indirect consequences resulting from the use of this book. The practices, exercises, and reflections contained herein are undertaken voluntarily and at the reader's own discretion and responsibility.

All quotations and references are included with sincere respect and acknowledgment of their sources.

Printed in Dunstable, United Kingdom

74135391R00145